OFF THE
ROAD
BROCK

£1.95

OFF THE ROAD BROCK

PETER BROCK

WITH WAYNE WEBSTER

IRONBARK
Pan Macmillan Australia

First published 1999 in Ironbark by Pan Macmillan Australia Pty Limited
St Martins Tower, 31 Market Street, Sydney

Reprinted 1999 (twice)

National Library of Australia
cataloguing-in-publication data:

Brock, Peter, 1945– .
Off the road, Brock: around Australia with Peter Brock.

ISBN 0 330 36173 2.

1. Brock, Peter, 1945– —Journeys. 2. Automobile rallies—Australia.
3. Automobile racing drivers—Australia. I. Webster, Wayne. II. Title.

796.730994

Typeset in 11.75/16pt Minion by Midland Typesetters
Printed in Australia by McPherson's Printing Group

CONTENTS

ROUTE MAP

INTRODUCTION

Thank you for the privilege of being so tired that death would be welcome. Thank you for my straining, red, stinging eyes desperately searching for a road through an oil-smeared windscreen on a slimy, muddy, snow-edged track in the high country, with my navigator screaming, 'Go! Go! Go!' And who can forget your car sliding towards the blackness at the edge of a 200-metre drop into nothing, the itching of my five-day-old beard ...

Thanks, I'll be there for the next one.

Letter from a competitor in the 1995
Round Australia Rally

There are those who would tell you that there is no adventure left in the world, that all the great mountains have been climbed, oceans sailed, continents explored and secrets uncovered. These cynics reckon that there are no challenges left in the world, that everything worth doing has been done.

Certainly, as we leap into the 21st century, it may appear at first glance that there is nothing left for the adventurer to attempt. These days, you can log into the right Internet site and explore the deepest jungles of the Amazon or the freezing wastes of Antarctica, taking a 'virtual' tour of those parts of the world where human habitation is still the exception rather than the rule.

But to say that adventure is dead and buried, and challenges are few and far between, is completely wrong. Just ask any of the 57 teams that lined up for the start of one of the great motoring adventures—the PlayStation Rally Round Australia 1998. Ask them if the course of this three-week epic, which circumnavigated the driest, oldest and most challenging continent on earth, is not one of the most imposing journeys remaining for those with the spirit of competition and a desire to tackle the unknown.

Australia is an amazing place. It can be both breathtakingly beautiful and brutally inhospitable. In parts, the temperature can soar above 40 degrees Celsius while only a few thousand kilometres away it can be below freezing. You want contrast? Australia is where you will find it.

The distances involved in trying to tame this continent by car are truly staggering. Some Australians have no idea just how vast their land really is, while many overseas visitors have the rather odd perception that, because Australia is an island, it's small. I remember a friend telling me about the time he was in Hong Kong and met a group of US sailors who had come ashore off their aircraft carrier. My friend shared a few beers with the Americans, who quizzed him about Australia as they were headed to Perth and looking forward to a little shore leave. But he really couldn't help them that much, being from Sydney. Not to worry, said the navy brigade as they departed, instead of just hanging around in Perth, they'd hire a car and drive to Sydney one afternoon and catch up for a drink.

They truly had no idea that Sydney is roughly 5000 km east of Perth—around the same distance Los Angeles is from New York.

And of course there is no shortage of stories—most I reckon belonging to the urban myth category—about tourists hailing a cab at Sydney airport and asking to be taken to Ayers Rock.

No, Australia is anything but compact. Sure, any modern vehicle that has been well maintained and is well prepared can cross the immense distances with relative ease (although it always pays to remember that in outback areas there can be vast distances between fuel outlets). Modern highways have opened up areas that once claimed the lives of brave and sometimes foolhardy explorers. Turn on the radio, crank up the air conditioning and you can travel nearly anywhere in Australia along a ribbon of bitumen in the kind of effortless comfort that belies the efforts of the original band of explorers who uncovered the secrets of the oldest continent.

But get off the beaten track, ignore the ribbons of bitumen, and you'll find Australia still has a wicked nature and the ability to bruise, batter and break the most well-prepared of adventurers. Treat this continent without respect and it will turn and savage you. This element of danger, allied to the challenges offered by the contrasting terrain, is why outback Australia remains a huge adventure for drivers. And it is why the PlayStation Rally captured my attention. Although I had retired from professional circuit driving, I always said that when a potentially exciting event came along then I'd give it a go.

Consequently, when Bruce Garland—something of an off-road racing legend having captured victory in the Australian Safari, an incredibly tough desert race—offered me a drive in one of his Holden Jackaroo four-wheel drives, I couldn't resist. Bruce was planning to prepare and enter two Jackaroos in the PlayStation Rally—his own specially modified version and a stock-standard model, backed by AMP, for me. A four-wheel drive, Bruce reckoned, was the way to go in an 18,000 km race around the nation and in his view the Jackaroo was the best of the breed. Given that he has rallied Jackaroos for years, I took him at his word.

In 1979 and again in 1995 I had competed in round-Australia trials, both times driving Holden Commodores. However, Bruce was sure that the pounding nature and the speed of the '98 version would play into the hands of the 4 × 4 runners—especially in the opening stages of the event, west from Adelaide, which were scheduled to pass through some pretty rough landscape.

No one had any doubts that there would be days when the more traditional rally cars—lighter, more nimble and faster over smooth stages—would have the upper hand. But the trick, Bruce argued, would be for the Jackaroos to make an early break and establish an unassailable lead. And, if we could get the cars to chase us, to push themselves up to and over their limits, many would break or be mortally wounded before the event reached the east coast and the smoother, more conventional rally roads.

I was joined in the Jackaroo by my navigator, Sydney motoring journalist Wayne Webster. 'Webby' and I have known each other for over 20 years, but he came into the PlayStation having only ever navigated once before. That was back in 1992, when he teamed up with my former Mobil Racing team-mate, Brad Jones, to contest the inaugural Targa Tasmania in a factory-entered Holden Commodore Group A SS. According to Webby, a driving error was the cause of their car slamming into a tree stump on the third stage of Day One, while Brad maintains it was a dud call from the navigator's side. The only time they've shared a vehicle since was during the ride to Devonport Hospital—in the ambulance that carted them away from the crash site.

Since then, Webby has stuck to steering. So before we

departed round Australia for three weeks, we decided to put the new partnership to the test. He wanted to find out if I could still drive after my retirement and I was keen to see if he could read a map. After all, he maintained he suffered from a rare form of directional dyslexia that often got him lost within his house. His initial strategy, that if we kept the ocean on the left we would be heading in the right direction, certainly had merit. However, such logic lacked the kind of detail that would be needed to stay in contention during what organisers were claiming would be the hardest, toughest and fastest round-Australia yet. Given just how brutal things had been in the 1979 and 1995 rallies, this was a big claim and one not to be taken lightly. That's why we decided to see if we could work together.

So on 18 July we ran ahead of the field for a part of the Bay Stages Rally, through the mountains near Batemans Bay on the far south coast of New South Wales. This was a round of the State Championship and the perfect way to have a blast and see how we gelled as a team. It also gave us the chance to put the Jackaroo through its paces, and developed into something of a learning experience for both of us. I had never driven a four-wheel drive in anger before and I admit to being stunned by the amount of traction on offer. Sure, the Jackaroo didn't have the out-and-out power of a purpose-built rally car, but it handled incredibly well and held its ground when cornering. Indeed, I could hardly believe the level of grip it offered in slippery situations. I left Batemans Bay wishing I had caught on to this four-wheel drive caper a lot earlier.

And Webby and I got on well together. As far as I was concerned, the three of us—Jackaroo, driver and navigator— were a good team for the PlayStation.

When I lined up for the start of the '98 PlayStation Rally

I had an additional objective to those that had motivated my other two round-Australia attempts. I wanted to enjoy the spirit of competition and to use the lap of the nation to say thank you to the fans around Australia who had supported me for so many years. I had managed to meet so many during my final season in the touring-car ranks, and indeed I was overwhelmed by the level of support I had received during that last year with the Mobil Holden Racing Team. But there were so many areas of Australia we didn't go to. The PlayStation Rally offered a unique opportunity to have a steer in an exciting event, to have some fun and to reach fans in the more remote regions of the country.

When I announced my retirement in 1997, saddling up for one last season with the Holden Racing Team, I was truly staggered by the response from fans. That I had somehow managed to touch the lives of so many people over the years was humbling, and here was a chance to say thank you. I was determined to offer as much of my time as humanly possible during the PlayStation to talk with fans, sign autographs and give something back to those who have followed my career with such unwavering dedication.

I'll never forget the last time I competed at Bathurst—that weekend in 1997 remains one of the most memorable times of my life. I was astounded by the level of crowd support that I received. I simply couldn't tally up the number of autographs I signed during that final fling at Bathurst; it seemed like the only time I wasn't signing my name was when I was strapped into the 05 Commodore and pounding around the greatest racetrack in the world.

It's strange how the public and the media blew everything up to such immense proportions during that last outing. No one, it seemed, was going to be happy without me leaving

Mt Panorama with a 10th Bathurst victory—the 'Perfect 10' they liked to call it—safely in my keeping.

However, I'd like to point out that it would have been *far* from a perfect 10. I raced at Mt Panorama 29 times and won nine times. Which means I lost 20 times. A perfect 10? I should be so lucky. Still, I did manage to win around one in every three races. However, never forget that motor racing is a team effort—the driver is an important cog, but even Michael Schumacher can't win if his car is parked by the side of the road with an expired engine. I was truly fortunate to have some brilliant people behind me for the majority of my career.

I've been in the game far too long to expect a fairytale ending, and although I led the race throughout my opening stint—and I could actually hear the crowd cheering on those first few laps over the roar of the engine—that 10th win wasn't to be. The engine of 05 cried 'Enough' just after co-driver Mark Skaife took over the driving duties. Around me the reaction was incredible. Some members of the team and many of the spectators were in tears. But rather than see that final race as the end of my career, I saw it as the start of the second part of my life, one which would hold as many challenges as the first.

When it comes to my career highlights, most people prefer to talk about Bathurst and, indeed, it has played a major role in taking me to where I am today. However, in many ways, one of the most satisfying moments of my career came not at Mt Panorama, but on the most demanding, intimidating and daunting circuit of them all ... Australia!

I'd have to say that the 1979 Repco Reliability Trial was the toughest, most brutal event I've ever been involved in. Competitors in that rally were expected to maintain average speeds that made sleep out of the question, drivers pushing their vehicles to the limit to make the target times. We were driving for three days straight, then we'd go for a short break, then maybe drive for another 48 to 60 hours again. It was outrageously difficult to do. Modern-day safety regulations would preclude that now.

A lot of critics thought my entry in that '79 round-Australia contest was nothing more than a publicity stunt. Their thinking was along the lines of 'how could a circuit racer ever hope to match some of the world's biggest rally stars?', especially when my team-mates in the Marlboro Holden Dealer Team Commodores included giants of the sport such as internationals Rauno Aaltonen and Shekar Mehta, and local rally stars such as Barry Ferguson and Wayne Bell. I was dismissed as a 'tar baby' who had managed to make the team simply to generate a little free publicity for the event. Everyone expected me to just make up the numbers. If ever I needed added motivation, this was it.

I was born on a farm and learnt to drive at the age of seven, out on the back paddock in an old Chev truck. From then on, I drove anything that had wheels on it—old tractors, utes, motorbikes, whatever. And, inevitably, a lot of that driving was done on loose surfaces. The PR machine for the Repco told the world that I was born and bred in the big city, a cocky young circuit racer who wanted to emulate Jack Brabham. But the truth is that I had an upbringing that had taught me how to cope with all sorts of driving conditions. I'd never done any rallies, but loose surfaces held no mysteries to me.

As it turned out, the Repco was fantastic, like a second childhood in a way. I sensed that the experienced rally drivers didn't like me winning too much. To some extent they still don't like it—I'm regarded as a driver who can go fast on rally drivers' dirt, but I'm not a rally driver, not one of them. And, to be honest, I don't see myself as one of them, not at all.

But I love going on long-distance rallies. When I did that '79 event, the greatest thing for me was that I got to experience a whole range of things that were totally different to what I was used to. The expectations, the pressure, the camaraderie—especially the camaraderie—were all different. In the cut and thrust of circuit racing, you never do things such as stopping to help fellow competitors, but that's part and parcel of rally driving. In rallies, if one of your rivals has broken down, you can and will stop to see how they are, and how you might be able to assist.

In a long-distance endurance event such as a round-Australia rally, you're all out there battling against the odds. Overnight, in a location far removed from city streets, you'll find a group of guys hanging around a campfire, sometimes shivering with cold, recalling where they've been and how they just got through, and looking forward to where they're about to go . . .

'Have you heard the creek's flooded!' one might say, to universal approval. This is not a setback, just another hurdle to eagerly overcome.

Around that campfire, everyone's trying to wind each other up. Not just drivers, but navigators and service crews too. The emphasis is very much on having a good and exciting time. And I loved to join in. But once I started down that road early the next morning, I was as committed as I'd ever been on a race circuit. You see, I only know one way. When I'm behind the wheel of a car, I approach the task in the same manner, whether I'm driving an old paddock bomb out the back of my property or rushing over the top of the mountain at Bathurst.

In 1979, and even in the '98 PlayStation, the standard of performance expected of me was less than it had been during my circuit career. To me that was neither a good nor a bad thing. I've never bothered about expectations. Whether I'm driving in front of an audience of two people or 10,000, my commitment is still the same. My motor racing philosophy has always simply been to get out there and have a red-hot go. Let's enjoy it. Let's take this machinery and belt it down this road, wherever it might be, and see what happens.

But it pays not to be foolhardy. The job is to get from here to there as quickly, effectively and efficiently as possible. Go *too* fast and you damage the car, maybe yourself as well. In a rally, if you hurt your vehicle, there might not be any spares up the road. Or you might not make it further up the road.

I always tried to turn the expectations of others, and potential barriers such as stress and fear of failure, into positives. When I lined up on the grid I always saw an opportunity. I saw my fans in the crowd and used their support to assist and inspire me, rather than thinking that if I made a mistake they'd desert me. Self-confidence is an amazing thing.

I remember when we set off on the Repco back in 1979 we had a couple of fishing rods strapped to the roof of the Commodore. It was a joke, even though fishing is one of my favourite leisure activities. Regardless, it was clear from Day One that we'd never get the chance to use them. With the kind of schedule that event organiser, the late Stewart McLeod, had set, the fish of Australia were very safe from the attention of the competitors in the 1979 Repco Trial.

Nineteen years later, and we headed into some remote areas

once more. It never ceased to amaze me that, even when we ended up in the middle of nowhere—standing at the side of a barely recognisable dirt track seemingly a million miles from civilisation—someone would wander up with a camera. They simply wanted to grab a photograph, or have an autograph book or a photo signed. Sometimes they just wanted a chat.

Some sportspeople think such requests are intrusive and resent it. I don't. Without the support of the fans where would any of us be? And I have to admit that the best part of what I do is meeting and enjoying a yarn with people. That's what it's all about.

I must confess I haven't had one moment of regret since I decided to leave circuit racing. Believe me, there's not a moment I would change, for life is all about what you make of it, and the choices I have made in the past—whether right or wrong—have been my choices and no one else's. These choices were always based on the best knowledge I had at the time. However, nothing stays the same, and what is appropriate at one time may not be at another.

Retiring from full-time racing wasn't a hard decision. It was simply that the time had come to do something else. I'd like to think I was still holding my own against the young guns of the sport, but there is always a very real trap of overstaying one's welcome—and that's a trap many sports-people fall into. For three decades, my life had revolved around driving cars, but I realised that the time had come to pursue other directions. I woke up one day and came to the realisation that if I didn't start to explore new avenues, to leave my comfort zone and try other things in the near future, opportunities could easily get away from me.

I'd like to think that everything I have experienced has happened in order to prepare me for my 'second life'. Ironically, since I gave it away I've never been so busy. Sometimes I think there are not enough hours in the day, but I am a person who can't stand still. It's in my nature to try different things, to try to get a handle on all things that life has to offer.

I've had the most amazing life and been privileged to share my life with so many people. Certainly, when I was just a young hopeful building my first car I could never have imagined what the future held for me.

I now have the luxury of being able to choose the events I want to tackle, ones that look like fun and offer the chance to do something different. And the 1998 PlayStation Rally certainly had all the right ingredients to satisfy those demands . . .

DAY 1

ADELAIDE
TO
PORT AUGUSTA

R ally enthusiasts—and a large number of other Aust- ralians—old enough to remember events such as the legendary Redex, Mobilgas, Repco and Ampol Trials will recall stories of the horrific conditions competitors faced during those events. They'll know, too, the folk heroes such as 'Gelignite' Jack Murray, Jack Davey, Eddie Perkins, Ken Tubman and many other larger-than-life characters who drove in them. A whole nation found itself caught up in the unique character of those famous races.

Back then, just driving around Australia on what were laughingly called 'highways' was a daunting test of grit, determination and sheer stamina—from man and machine. Obviously the roads have improved immensely since those daredevil days. 'Progress' has meant that now most drivers can journey around this great country of ours in their family vehicle on decent roads, find a nice bed and dinner each night at a motel or roadhouse, and never see a dirt road. However, while Australia is now ringed by all-weather black-top roads, many of those old Redex tracks still remain. Sometimes only a few metres away from the new bitumen roads, many of Aus- tralia's original highways lie all but unused and in a state of ever-worsening disrepair. Some are now little more than faint wheel tracks in the mulga; a few, though, are surprisingly well preserved. Some no longer appear on maps. Many are simply cattle or sheep station tracks.

Anyone arriving at the starting line for the 1998 PlayStation Round Australia Rally looking for a comfortable cruise around the nation was sadly out of luck. The ambition of organisers was to recapture that spirit of adventure, camaraderie and ultra-tough competition that were the hallmark of the famous rallies of yesteryear.

The plan was to cover 18,300 km in 22 days. On average,

almost 900 km—more than the distance between Sydney and Melbourne—per day. The race would leave Adelaide on September 6. Early spring was considered to be the time of year when the weather around on the country is most settled, when rain in the southern part of Australia would be unlikely to cause any damage to the roads and tracks on which the rally would take place.

Bob Carpenter, the Clerk of the Course, began planning for the PlayStation in October 1997, setting out on a preliminary survey in a Toyota LandCruiser. That initial survey took five-and-a-half weeks to complete, during which time Carpenter and Assistant Clerk of the Course, Jim Reddiex, set out to find challenging tracks that would create a modern rally embodying the trials and tribulations of the past. They wanted the Play-Station to provide the ultimate challenge.

Carpenter had cut his rallying teeth in an old Mobilgas trial, but really got caught up in rallying in club and state championship rallies, driving a Morris Major and then a Mini Cooper S in the 1960s. He's been directing the Australian Safari since 1986. Reddiex was part of the all-Australian team that won the London to Munich World Cup Rally in a Citroen in 1974, an event that covered over 10,000 km and battled through horror sections in the Sahara Desert. He also competed in many round-Australia and Australian Safari events, including partnering Andrew Cowan in the 1979 Repco.

There aren't many roads in Australia that Carpenter and Reddiex don't know about.

Before they set off on their initial survey, Carpenter had looked over his dusty collection of maps and rediscovered old main roads and other tracks that had faded due to lack of use, or are now ignored because new roads have been built. The pair pondered new possibilities each day and investigated each region before seeking out the property owner or local Aboriginal community to explain what the round-Australia was all about. Every metre of every special stage had to be covered by written permission, either from the landholder or lessee in the case of private land, Forestry offices in the case of State forests, Shire Councils in the case of closed shire roads, Land Councils and Aboriginal community elders in the case of any Aboriginal land, State governments in the case of Crown Land, and so on and so on.

After that initial survey, Carpenter and Reddiex set off again in a Toyota diesel-powered LandCruiser the following February for the more detailed second phase of finalising the route chart, measuring the distances accurately and planning the start and finish points of each stage. In late June, the pair did their third circumnavigation in order to do a final course check, this time accompanied by CAMS-appointed course checker Stewart Lister and another CAMS official, Stuart Kostera. This final course check saw the LandCruiser joined by a conventional Toyota Camry wagon, which was taken to ensure that two-wheel drive cars, particularly the historic competitors, would be able to get through all stages.

In short, the organisers had left no stone unturned—literally—in their quest to develop a course that would mean those who returned to Adelaide three weeks later would have achieved something great. This would be a rally where simply finishing would be a victory in itself ...

I remember how I felt before the Repco rally in 1979. It was going to be a huge adventure, something that I'd never done before in my life. I didn't have any idea of what I was getting myself in for. As it turned out, that event developed into the single most arduous activity I had ever undertaken in my life. And to win it was the single most memorable achievement of my life in motorsport.

I knew then that if I could drive the car around and not get into any strife, then I'd do all right. Same with this one. I kept reminding myself: keep the car out of trouble and we'll be okay.

Get on the road, drive as well as I can, and then look back and say, 'Hey, we're doing all right'. That's all I wanted to worry about. No need to worry about how anyone else was going. No need to get ahead of myself. In a sense, it doesn't matter what might be down the road, worry about what's now.

Bob Carpenter had promised that the PlayStation would be the toughest round-Australia endurance test of modern times. This sounded perfect, as I love events that are a huge examination for a driver. Just being able to compete for two or three weeks is a real challenge of stamina and skill. Bob told me that for just the first survey of the course he'd spent 52 days on the road, covered a total of 26,500 km, used nearly 3000 litres of petrol and changed and repaired 20 flat tyres. He reckoned, too, that he'd opened and closed around 1500 gates, visited 120 outback cattle and sheep stations, made hundreds of new friends and murdered four million flies and mosquitoes.

I hadn't driven our Jackaroo since Batemans Bay. A big, high thing, it had good vision and felt okay. But is it fast? Not, I thought, compared to some of the hot Commodores I've driven in the past. Other cars tackling the event ranged from a squadron of finely-prepared four-wheel drives, some very rapid rally cars including the Commodores used by Ross

Dunkerton and me in the 1995 round-Australia and an amazing selection of veteran vehicles including a couple of late '60s Monaros, a 1972 LJ Torana GTR XU1 and, perhaps most baffling of all, a 1966 Morris Mini Cooper S.

A lot of familiar faces—drivers, navigators and support crew members—turn up for these events. 'We haven't missed one!' they'll explain, as they vigorously shake your hand.

It's hard to say that someone is the 'typical rally driver'. In fact, these men and women come from all walks of life. Many have taken their month's annual leave. Some are doctors, or public servants—people you look at and think, 'How meek and mild are they?' But they're 'Clark Kents', dashing from the telephone booth to their trusty vehicle, eyeballs spinning, ready for their next big adventure in the bush. So skilful are these rare individuals at keeping their cars on the road and moving forward that they never get disheartened.

The guys in the Mini, Doug Coote and Cono Onofaro, are good examples of such characters. So are Alan Cameron and Ted Rogers, who ran the Torana XU1. The Torana is a tough little car, but, though the blokes will be upset to read it, it's not a vehicle suited to round-Australia rallying. Outback Australia? Torana XU1? Creek crossings? Limited suspension? No!!

I know how hard it is to compete in a round-Australia event driving a modern, purpose-built rally vehicle. To line up for a three-week epic, which would cross some of the toughest country in the world, in a tiny car that had seen many years go by since it first rolled off the production line, borders on the heroic.

However, it was David Lowe and Robert Gambino, in their 1973 Datsun 180B SSS, who really struck me as being very clever. Right from the jump, they would never run the car too hard. They had virtually no service crew. In fact, their entire support consisted of one of the guy's wives and another bloke's best mate. For spare parts they did the best they could with what was available in the next town.

Some other guys went at it like the proverbial bat out of hell, from minute one. They'd get away with it for a while, maybe nine times out of 10, but eventually, they'd come unstuck.

Barry Ferguson, driver of one of our three HDT Commodores on the 1979 Repco Trial and a bit of a legend in rally circles, had entered in the PlayStation in a 1976 Volkswagen Beetle. The honour for having the oldest car in the field belonged to John Anderson, who had rolled out a 1955 Peugeot 203. Anderson had competed in a '55 Peugeot in the 1995 round-Australia, winning the Historic Under 1300cc Class despite rallying without a back-up service crew and rolling the vehicle on the highlands inland from Wauchope in northern New South Wales. They needed help from Peugeot Club members and handymen around the country to get the car to the finish line, but get there they did!

No matter what the vehicle, be it an outright contender or one that would earn accolades by simply making it all the way around, the one thing all competitors had in common was their adventurous spirit. The experience was going to fuel stories that would keep dinner parties entertained for years to come.

The pre-event favourite had to be Bruce Garland, my Jackaroo team-mate. Bruce runs his own business in Sydney, building and preparing not only his own rally Jackaroos, but those of other competitors as well. For the PlayStation, Bruce had painstakingly built himself a brand new Jackaroo in T1 specifications, which meant it had a reinforced chassis, dual shock absorbers on each wheel, a hotted-up engine and a competition gearbox with special ratios, all housed in a lightweight body shell.

Having already won the Australian Safari, which is considerably shorter than a round-Australia trial but run over consistently tough country, raced successfully in the 1997 Dubai Desert Safari and led his class during the 1998 Paris to Dakar, Bruce reckoned he had the goods to be at the front of the field. As far as he was concerned, the harder the better. As usual, his navigator was Harry Suzuki, who has been calling directions for Bruce for some time now and is one of the best in the business. Harry is as subtle as Bruce is loud. Then again, compared with Bruce's laugh, a 747 at takeoff is whisper quiet.

Bruce is an absolute classic. A modern-day Jack Murray if you like. Ask him about the Dubai race and he can't help grinning, like a groom looking back on his wedding day ...

'It was like a scene from Indiana Jones,' he remembers enthusiastically, 'with Arabs and camels waiting on the other side of *huge* sand hills as the cars came flying over the top!'

He's always getting up to some sort of prank. Word has it that during a Christmas party at his suburban workshop, he built a mobile swimming pool by cutting the roof off an old station wagon and lining the now-exposed interior with a plastic tarp. As he approached the start of the PlayStation, on Rundle St in the middle of Adelaide, he was seen lobbing firecrackers out of his window—a throwback to the days of Gelignite Jack—to the delight of the crowd behind the ropes. Bruce laughs a lot and out loud. People love him. And he's recognised as being the archetypal rally driver.

'Bring on more rocks, bring on more mud, bring on more

dust,' he'll implore organisers. 'Bring on rougher roads, more drama.'

He laughs—*laughs*—about hitting boulders at 160 km an hour and the car caving in around him. His crew'll stretch it back again, and then he'll go looking for another boulder. If he was a golfer, he'd aim for the bunkers.

I like Bruce, I like him a lot. He's very clever and a very good driver. He might like to pretend that he doesn't care too much, but he does. He inevitably gets a little nervous beforehand and is forever making last-minute changes—shifting things about, maybe jettisoning a few things he now considers unnecessary, just to lighten the load, maybe losing a little fuel, no need to carry anything you don't need. Bruce's automotive garage in Sydney pays the rent, but rallies are what matters. If there's a major rallying event on, then there is no way the garage is going to get in the way. He's an uncomplicated, charitable soul with a great love of life, who does what he wants to do. And when he does it, he never loses sight of his objectives and tries his best to do the job well.

A genuine character, he's known throughout the rally game as 'Bruce the Goose'. As far as he's concerned, rallying is a caper, an adventure. But don't think he's silly. No way! Bruce is simply a man who won't let anyone or any situation get in the way of a good time. Travelling around Australia, no matter what environment he finds himself in, he fits in. Once a stage is over, he'll grab his old bush hat, go for a bit of a wander. Sure enough, he'll soon be striking up a conversation, maybe learning a bit about life and the bush from a group of locals, maybe discovering a little about the conditions he'll be facing in the morning.

Also entrusting their hopes of victory in Garland-built

Jackaroos were Ross Nicastri, who had purchased one of Bruce's old competition models for the PlayStation, and Queensland Holden dealer Peter Lockhart, who was driving a brand new '98 model.

Bruce's support crew was made up of motor racing people using their annual holidays to live out this latest adventure. And loving it! Sleeping out every night in swags, cooking up a storm in the bush, following the rally up to a 1000 km a day for three weeks running, just to work on the cars. Up until at least 10 o'clock at night, then awake again at 3.00 am. They follow the rally in trucks so slow that they have to set off that early in the morning just to reach the next base in time to meet their cars, and to be prepared for whatever emergency might arise. Perhaps new tyres need to be located, or an expert found to correct another unexpected problem. You need enormous commitment to fill this role, and you also need a leader who is able to command enormous loyalty. Bruce Garland is such a skipper.

There's no fear of failure in Bruce's crew, only a love of what they're doing and a commitment to the team. More a bushie's philosophy than a city slicker's way of thinking, I'd reckon.

This is the type of spirit that rallying engenders. To a large extent, rallying is the backbone of what we like to think are 'fair dinkum' Aussies. It's the spirit of John Williamson's song, *True Blue*. Probably what John Howard meant when he included the term 'mateship' in his preamble to the Constitution. These are people who want no more out of life than the satisfaction that comes from helping their comrades out.

There isn't that same feeling in circuit racing. Maybe elements of it, but never does it pervade as much as it does in rallying. During an endurance rally, if you see someone on the side of the track needing assistance, you stop and offer some assistance. You never want to get in a 'them against us' scenario, because inevitably, sooner or later, you're going to need them. You really need people to be prepared to give each other a hand.

Placing their faith in a modified Mitsubishi Pajero were New South Wales panel beater Warren Ridge, and his navigator, wife Joy. Warren just loves his off-road rallying; over the course of three weeks I don't think I ever saw him without a smile on his face. Reg Owen, from Warrnambool in Victoria, was flying the Nissan flag in his Patrol, while another husband-and-wife team, Ian and Val Swan, were hoping to prevent Holden's third straight round-Australia victory in their Ford Explorer.

Inevitably, there was a clash of ideas about the best way to tackle the '98 PlayStation. However, most agreed with Bruce Garland that the initial stages of the event, through South Australia, Western Australia and the Northern Territory, would play into the hands of the four-wheel drives, which would be better able to deal with the punishing conditions. And just as many reckoned that when the field reached Queensland for the run down the east coast, the tide would swing in favour of conventional passenger cars. There was no doubting that without a significant ground clearance, the passenger cars would struggle when the going got tough, but on the smoother east-coast run they would finally be able to utilise their speed advantage over the 4 × 4s.

The biggest danger to the Jackaroos, in many people's eyes, was the Subaru WRX of rally ace Michael Guest, who had arrived in Adelaide to join the car's owner, Jason Walk, for the trip. As Michael has proved, by winning the Group N class in two world championship rallies in Australia and New

Zealand against some of the finest drivers in the world, he's stunningly quick and incredibly committed. And as he showed when finishing second in the 1995 round-Australia, driving a Mitsubishi Galant VR4, he has what it takes to go the distance in a gruelling endurance event. Michael had only committed to the drive in August, after media speculation he might be competing in a Mazda RX-7 Turbo.

Although the WRX was a Group N car, which meant it was closer to standard than the full world rally championship missiles driven by the likes of world champion Colin McRae, it would still have the ability to easily outrun one of the four-wheel drives in smooth conditions. However, the way it sat hunched close to the ground meant that in the really tough stuff Guest would have to be very circumspect or risk inflicting some pretty heavy damage on his vehicle.

Also not to be discounted were the two Pedders-backed Holden Commodore utes of suspension guru Ron Pedder who was teamed with his son Scott, and rally ace Graeme Wise who had Linda Long handling the navigating chores. Wise and Pedder had tested their vehicles during the Saxon Safari in Tasmania earlier in the year, and pronounced themselves confident of a good showing in the round-Australia.

My mount for the PlayStation was a Bruce Garland-prepared vehicle, but instead of running in the modified class, it would run in stock-standard trim. Of course, it had the usual safety modifications such as competition seats, six-point harness belts, a roll cage and a fully encapsulated, competition fuel tank. However, the engine was just as it left the factory, as was the gearbox.

Bruce made it perfectly clear that without the benefit of a strengthened chassis, the Jackaroo would have to be driven carefully to avoid dangerous stress fractures from the pounding it would receive over the 21 days of competition. He also stressed that the car would lack the speed and punch out of the corners of its modified rivals. Considering this, I thought we could challenge for a top-10 position—maybe even a top-five place if there was a little attrition along the way—but a repeat of my '79 victory would be most unlikely . . .

But not impossible.

The organisers of the PlayStation Rally, Advantage International, decided to start the event in Adelaide because the South Australian government showed a desire to be involved. Still smarting over losing the rights to stage the Australian Formula One Grand Prix to Victoria, South Australia has moved to try to attract more top-level motorsport. They realise what a positive impact such events can have, both economically and on the State's morale.

Adelaide is one of my favourite cities. It runs at a slower pace than Melbourne or Sydney and the locals are quite enthusiastic about their sport—be it the hugely-successful Adelaide Crows in the AFL or the start of a round-Australia rally. There was a big roll-out for the start of the PlayStation and I was kept busy signing autographs, chatting with fans and doing a live cross for Channel 7's *Sportsworld* program. In fact I was so busy I almost didn't make it back to the Jackaroo for the start, and given that I had the honour of leading the field away, that would have been a quite a faux pas.

The first casualty of the event was the Ford Explorer of Ian and Val Swan, which refused to fire up for the short hop from the hotel to the starting line. They did manage to get the vehicle going, but were to suffer similar problems at the end of the first stage. We discovered later that their car's black box engine management computer had suffered a terminal mental breakdown, leaving the big off-roader temporarily stranded in the driveway. Unfortunately, motorsport can be like that; if I've learned anything in all my years of racing, it's that you have to roll with the punches.

Remarkably, Ian and Val went out and bought an old Falcon ute so they could continue around Australia as a support vehicle for the other Swan Explorer, driven by Steve and Stewart Cornwall.

Despite the fact that we started at the head of the field, when we reached the start of the first competitive stage— appropriately called 'First Blood'—around two hours after leaving Adelaide, we were slotted back into our seeded position of fifth.

The first of four opening-day stages, this was just a 29 km blast to let the field taste a little dust, a fast-flowing dash over some quick shire roads surrounded by farmland. The route instructions pointed out—as if it was needed—that an 18,000 km rally cannot be won on Day One. But it can be lost. It's all too easy to get carried away at the start of an event and let a rush of blood force out common sense. In a daunting event such as this, only the strongest survive, and without a healthy vehicle in the dying stages of the event there would be no chance of victory.

So for the opening two stages, the second being a short but challenging 24 km run offering a taste of the outback rallying to come, it was a case of look before you leap. And that's another trick to a round-Australia trial. Because of the sheer distances involved, you learn very quickly that it is impossible for those who set the course to warn competitors, through the printed route instructions, about each and every bump, hump and jump.

In sprint rallies, it's different, but in a round-Australia you have to be able to read the road and drive to the conditions that you see through the windscreen. (Of course, when you're swallowing the dust of a car in front you can't always see the road, which adds to the degree of difficulty.) But if every hazard were recorded, the route instruction book for each day would be roughly the size of the A-K and L-Z Sydney phone books combined.

The first service stop of the day was in Jamestown. I reckon just about every one of the 1300 or so inhabitants had turned out to greet the crews. Webby immediately headed towards the food stalls set up by the locals, while I attempted to satisfy the horde of autograph seekers who surrounded the Jackaroo service area. There was no shortage of people lining up for an autograph and, as always, the hospitality we received was brilliant.

The third competitive stage was another short leg, just 16 km. Then we ended the opening day of the event with a superb stage. It started on a shire laneway, which became what was basically two wheel tracks that went up and down a narrow ridge, forcing their weaving way between sharp, spiky, jagged rocks. If you slid sideways into a corner and hit these 'Stanley knives on rocks', you'd wreck both tyre and wheel. At times we raced down hills with a sheer precipice on one side, 100 metres to the bottom, sliding through corners on loose rubble. Over the edge and the only way you could survive would be to turn the fall into a drive down a cliff face and hope that you bounced over a few things and made it safely to the bottom. In other words, you were history.

Finally, we drove over to the east side of the Flinders Ranges. It was magnificent country, and the view from the top of the last hill was picture-postcard stuff. No wonder the rally organisers had called this stage 'Top of the World'. The

Jackaroo popped over the top of the ridge line and there, in full view to my right, was Spencer Gulf. As we came to that crest I was torn between catching a glimpse of the Gulf as the sun prepared to sneak beneath the mountains, and keeping a close eye on the other side, at the rocks, and danger! I'd be speeding along, as fast as I dared, and as often as I dared I'd sneak a peek at this spectacular sunset.

If the view of Spencer Gulf was breathtaking so too was the blast down the hill towards the end of the stage. The Jackaroo's speedo had us up to 170 km/h, but if others were to be believed, we must have been closer to 190 km/h. They reckoned that's what they were doing, but the official records confirmed that we had been going faster than they were.

It was on this part of the stage that Bruce Garland, pre-competition favourite, ran out of fuel. His doing so confirmed that Bruce was more serious about winning the rally than I'd given him credit for. Before I quickly tell this yarn, I must stress that in an endurance event such as the PlayStation, you're not allowed to get service on the road. If you run out of fuel on the highway and have to call for service, chances are you're going to cop a huge penalty. However, a competitor is allowed to stop to help another, if he or she chooses to. We're all competitors and we can do what we want to.

Ever since we'd first discussed the rally, Bruce had been this happy-go-lucky, hey-Brockie-let's-all-have-a-good-time sort of bloke. We knew that Bruce's car was running on a completely different gear ratio to my car and therefore he didn't have the luxury of cruising up the highway as I could; he had a car that was geared for flat-out rallying. Plus he had a number of engine modifications, all of which meant he was using up fuel at a greater rate than we were. But we didn't know at this point that he was also running on lighter fuel loads, whereas we were just filling up and going for it. No point, we thought, in being too scientific and trying to carry no more fuel than what was needed.

Bruce ran out of fuel ... a long way from Port Augusta. When we found him, we still had something like 40 litres left in our tank. He wasn't saying much, except that he wasn't going to make it. So we stopped to assist him.

We opened up the fuel system in our car, switched on the fuel pumps and blasted the fuel out of our fuel injection system into his tank. It took about 10 minutes to do the whole thing, after which Bruce told us to get going, he'd be all right. We arrived in Port Augusta with about three or four minutes in reserve, but Bruce arrived, breathless, with about 10 seconds to spare and, probably no more than the odd drop still in his fuel tank. On that very first day, he could have found himself right back down the field.

All that remained on Day One was a run along the highway into Port Augusta, a city that sits at the crossroads of the nation. From here, you can head north to Darwin, west towards Perth, south to Adelaide or east to Sydney.

The most surprising thing about Day One was that we had finished in second place outright, two minutes behind the hard-charging Guest in his Subaru. We hadn't expected to be leading the more highly modified four-wheel drives of Garland and Nicastri.

It seemed the stock-standard Holden had a bit more pace than everyone had believed.

DAY 2

PORT AUGUSTA
TO
EUCLA

'There's only one good road across the Nullarbor,' Bruce Garland had told *Australian Rallysport News* before the start of the 1998 round-Australia, 'and it's not the one we'll be taking!'

If Day One of the PlayStation Rally had been little more than a teaser of things to come, the dawn of Day Two heralded the moment when things would start to get serious. From now on the event would truly begin, for it was entering an intimidating stretch through the Nullarbor, Western Australia and the Northern Territory that would in all likelihood shape the final outcome.

There were to be four special stages on Day Two, including some longer stages across the kind of terrain that would make it clear to the 'sprinters' in the field that it's often smarter to be a 'stayer'. Horses don't win the Melbourne Cup if they can only run the first 1600 m before running out of puff. The process of sorting the men from the boys was set to begin in earnest.

Because I was trying to juggle my many commitments and also prepare for the event, before the rally started, I hadn't given the concept of 'seeding' or how the organisers would work out each day's starting order any great thought. To be honest, it didn't overly concern me because I didn't think the pace of the Jackaroo was going to be a factor. Consequently, I was pleasantly surprised when, after the first day, we were second quickest in the field. But even then the penny didn't really drop ...

'What's our starting position today?' I asked when I arrived for the beginning of Day Two.

'Oh, up there! *That's* pretty good,' I remarked when told we'd be second away. The idea of us being up the front of the grid, ahead of the cars that I considered the main contenders, had seemed pretty fanciful. I remember thinking, 'Beauty, I won't be driving in all those blokes' dust!'

I'm not trying to sound cocky. It's just that it wasn't until this moment that I truly realised that I was in a quick car, that I'd underestimated the Jackaroo. I had never harboured any thoughts of being in competition with all the other cars, that I could beat them *all*. My only ambition regarding the Jackaroo and the PlayStation was to get the absolute utmost out of my car, always keeping in mind that we had to get back to Adelaide in one piece. As events would turn out we were quickest on a number of stages during the rally, but the curious thing was that we were never the first car on the road two days running. Whenever we were first away, we'd invariably do something crazy, such as getting ourselves temporarily lost.

And we certainly never reached the point where we felt we could drive along as though we owned any particular piece of Australia.

After the field left Port Augusta we headed west for the sheep property of Siam, where the first two special stages of the day were to be run. The first was a 54 km dash along station tracks, sometimes vague and hard to see, with a few creek crossings thrown in just to keep things interesting. The second, 90 km stage was, in some parts, real pedal-to-the-metal stuff while in other areas the track wound itself around in such a maze that one had to take time to follow the arrows and keep to the correct path.

Of course, in this type of rally environment, your navigator is a key player. The navigator is in charge of direction. He or she has the map and advises when a turn is approaching, or a creek crossing, or a fork in the road. But it's not the navigator's job to tell the driver how to drive, or what gear to take, or what speed to aim for. No way. Rather it's the driver's job to make sure the navigator's concentration is sharp and thinking is clear ...

Say we're facing a track only wide enough for just one Jackaroo. 'Hey Webby, you know we're up to 140, 145, 150 ks,' I'd chuckle as we screamed along a sandy two-wheel track straight past a fence on one side and a line of overhanging trees on the other. Occasionally, we were brushing past leafy branches, relieved that we'd remembered to push the mirrors in before the stage began. We needed those centimetres on either side to get through at top speed. All Webby had to do was hold on tight and let me know when the next significant bend in the road was approaching.

Each day the navigator received notes from the rally Clerk of the Course and his assistants; these were complemented to some extent by any information we might have gleaned from the locals before the stage began. From either source, we might be told of stock in the vicinity of the road. Or that a creek has recently been washed away, so that instead of a 'caution' advice we were now facing a 'double caution'.

It's funny how whenever you discuss upcoming station tracks with the locals you discover that just about every road you're about to confront is the roughest road in Australia. 'You've seen rough roads?' proud locals will look at you quizzically. 'Mate, you wait to you get on these roads.'

Local knowledge is a guide, but never gospel.

Of course, the rally course had been surveyed more than once in the weeks and months before our adventure began. The track is always 'specked' once more the day before the rally passes through, and again an hour before. One of the rally organisers, in what we call the 'zero' car, drives through and then radios back, giving any special instructions as to what perils to expect. The track isn't open for competition until the zero car has been through and it has been closed to the public.

If on that final checkup they find something significantly different to the existing driving instructions, they'll let you know. Most times, though, they'll just tell you, 'Okay guys, you're on your own, sort yourselves out'.

So you'll set off, and not long into the trip you'll charge, way too fast, into a creek bed, fly though the air, the car will yell and scream, and you'll politely ask the navigator, 'Was there any caution on that one?' The navigator, a little shakily, will reply, 'Nuh!' And you'll think, 'What the hell was that zero car doing? He must have been going through there at 40 km/h.'

And you were doing more like 140!

A lot of the special stages would be held on old, now disued highways, station tracks or mining exploration roads. The latter two can be anything from a well-kept entrance into a homestead to no more than just two vague wheel tracks, which might have seen a mower in the previous months.

The terrain we faced on Day Two was inevitably flat station tracks. By now, we were well beyond the Flinders Ranges and racing on flat countryside littered with rocky outcrops of shale and limestone. Creek crossings, mulga and saltbush were scattered throughout. The trees were neither tall nor plentiful so, even when the track meandered through the bushes, visibility wasn't bad.

A station track is simply that, a rough-and-ready path across a station that might have first been blazed many decades before. Some appear to go in a particular direction for no reason at all—perhaps the track once swung around a tree long since gone. Perhaps it follows cow tracks. There's no drainage, no culverts. When you approach a creek crossing, if it's marked on your maps, you always slow down, but that crossing might have been preceded by a piece of road on which you were doing 150 km/h. Although you can usually spot a creek crossing by some telltale signs—an old fence post, a now disused windmill or certain species of trees that grow only where it's damp—it still might catch you unawares. In this country, however, more than damp spots, there's a lot of dust. You never sit right behind the car in front, because you won't be able to see the rocks or bends in the track, let alone the number plate and sponsorship of the driver ahead.

How then, do you get past slower cars? Simple in theory: you call the driver on the two-way radio. On special stages there might be anywhere between 10 and 50 cars on various parts of the road at a time, and all tuned to the one channel, channel 8. However, because of the limitations of the reach of the radio transmission, the drivers and navigators up front can't hear the blokes at the rear; you can only hear the cars in your immediate vicinity.

You might be driving along and coming up behind, say, car No 17. You know it's No 17 because that was the car that set off immediately before you. You get them on the radio, and ask them exactly where they are on the road. It's probably the first indication they've had that you've been closing in.

'About 48.6 km along the track,' they might reply.

'We're 47.8, and starting to cop a bit of dust,' we'll crackle over the two-way. 'Would you mind moving over?'

And they usually do. The rally camaraderie again.

But not always. Amongst rally drivers there is a running joke that radio signals don't go forward, that you can always hear radio messages from the cars in front of you, but never from behind. One day technology might fix this, but I doubt it.

Radio messages are also used to alert fellow drivers to potential hazards up ahead, such as stock on the road. If there's two tonne of dirty, big, angry, red bull on the road, and he is not happy, we'd like to know about it, thank you.

In the middle of a special stage, we could be given 400 to 800 m of track where the speed limit is 40 km/h or 50 km/h. This is a 'quiet' zone, which is strictly enforced, as the speed restriction may have been set during the negotiations to allow the station track to be included in the route. It might be, for example, a homestead area, or a shearing area, and we have to keep the noise right down as we go through. The last thing the owner of a property wants is for their front yard to be ripped to shreds by marauding rally cars, or for their main living areas to be covered in thick dust. If any car ignores these restrictions, then we've lost the trust of the station owner. So there is someone there monitoring cars' speeds (most of the time), with penalties for those who exceed the limit. This quiet zone can mean you've got a stage when otherwise you wouldn't have one.

On Day Two, a change to a shearing schedule meant that we had to make a detour around one area of a farm, splitting the planned first special stage into two stages. The first service stop of the day was at the Mt Ive station, a property run by the Andrew family. Merv, Joan and Peter Andrew are no strangers to motorsport, having graciously opened the gates of their property to a number of rallies in recent times. In fact, their association with speed-related things goes much further. Mt Ive is within spitting distance of Lake Gairdner, a giant saltpan (at least when there's no water) which has been used as the site of a number of land speed campaigns. It was here, for example, that Rosco McGlashan brought his jet-powered racer to have a shot at the land speed world record. So Mt Ive has become a popular place to be used as a base camp for these land speed crusades.

After the break, and an $80 drink of fuel for the thirsty Jackaroo, it was time to tackle the longest stage of the rally yet, a 115 km journey that had a bit of everything: gravel, sand, creek crossings, gullies and gates.

Some of it was very, *very* fast! In other places there was potential to rip the guts out of the vehicle thanks to some giant washaways created during the recent wet season. It was the kind of stage that demanded the complete attention of the driver and lots of common sense, and one where 'over driving' could have cost more than lost time.

The fourth and final special stage of the day was to have been a tough 120 km dash across the Old Eyre Highway. Now corrugated to the point that no tooth fillings would have been safe, the condition of this now rarely-used track is just what competitors back in the legendary round-Australia trials of the 1950s and '60s would have encountered day in and day out during their epic journeys. From the moment we arrived at the start of the stage—on a track which sat only a few hundred metres away from the smooth and fast bitumen road that is now the main highway—and looked out at the state of the first few hundred metres, it was easy to appreciate just how tough and determined those adventurers must have been over 40 years ago.

I was really looking forward to the 'blast'. Again, we were set to start second on the stage behind Michael Guest. With 120 km of hard slog ahead of us, much better suited to the Jackaroo than Michael's Subaru Impreza, he was quick to point out that if we caught him, all we had to do was get on the radio and he'd move out of our way. A brief description of the stage in the notes had convinced the young rally hard-charger that this would be the kind of country where cars with a higher ground clearance would have a clear advantage. Less suited vehicles would have to go slow in the tough terrain, to ensure they survived to fight another day.

The majority of the stage ran through Yalata Aboriginal country. Bob Carpenter had gained permission from the tribal elders to run the rally through their land but even with the best planning, not everything can be foreseen. Just as we were counting down for the start, Guest already at the line in his helmet and revving the engine of the Subaru, we saw a small cloud of dust appear in the distance, slowly heading towards us. As it drew closer, we saw it was a Toyota LandCruiser, filled with locals.

The rally track had just been closed to traffic, so the sight of a Toyota LandCruiser coming up in the opposite direction was just about the last thing we expected. Someone asked one of the blokes in the car what was going on, and he explained that there had been a funeral, down the road and off the track. There were a few more mourners still to come out of the bush and head back towards town. We'd just come from town.

It was such a long stage, and would have been a real car-breaker, so it was a shame to lose it, but out of respect to the local community we decided to abandon it. Webby and I reckoned we had just the right suspension and subtle setup to handle the massive corrugations on the old highway, more so than cars whose suspensions were rock hard. Nevertheless, we had no alternative but to turn around, rejoin the highway and make the run down the bitumen to the town of Eucla, where the service crews would be waiting and we would bed down for the night.

The trips between special stages are called 'transport stages'. On such stages, your ambition is simply to reach the end of the stage within the time allowed. No prizes for getting there early, but penalties if a stop for a sandwich or a toilet break goes over time and you arrive a little late. The race organisers don't want you to speed on a public highway so they give you ample time. But they don't want you to muck around either.

Eucla was originally the site for a repeater station for the overland telegraph system; operators working in a stone cottage took down messages from the eastern states and then relayed them to Perth, over 1400 km to the west. It's hardly a tourist destination, consisting of a petrol station, a motel, and a restaurant and bar.

This is tough, hard, uncompromising country, but it's not all desolation, for on the way into Eucla the highway runs alongside the southern edge of Australia. This is where Australia just ends. Full stop. Massive cliffs drop more than vertically into the pounding ocean far, far below. With time up our sleeve before we had to check in at the Eucla overnight point, we took a small detour to one of the many lookouts that dot the coastline.

We weren't the only ones to take advantage of the opportunity, for as we drove into the lookout we encountered the Pedder's service crew. And another couple, travelling in a motor home, had stopped to try to temporarily wipe away the effects of the energy-sapping heat of the Nullarbor crossing. I was just walking away from the edge of the cliff—the edge that I gladly admit to approaching on my hands and knees—when the woman from the motor home approached.

'You know,' she said flatly, 'you look just like Peter Brock.'

I had to admit that I was indeed guilty, which sparked an unscheduled photo call on the cliff's edge. I think they were a little baffled at how, in the middle of the Nullarbor, they had somehow run into a retired racing driver. And, despite an explanation, I'm still not sure that either the woman or her partner really grasped the concept of just what a round-Australia rally really involved. In fact, we waved them goodbye reasonably sure they believed we were on nothing more than a long-distance sightseeing trip around the continent. In a way, that was right—it was just that most of our sightseeing would be conducted at a significantly faster pace than usual.

After we reached Eucla, we learnt of the mishaps that had befallen a couple of our rivals. New South Welshmen Garry FitzGerald and John Noble had rolled their 1975 Datsun 240Z, while running 10th outright during Stage One. And the 1969 Monaro of Victorians Michael Holloway and Tim Kennon had hit a kangaroo at nearly 140 km/h later in the day. The Monaro, we were told, was fine. The roo was less than healthy.

Another car to introduce itself to a roo was the old Falcon ute of Ian and Val Swan. Remember they only took possession of this car the day before, after their Ford Explorer had to retire. No one was game to go near them now!

At the close of play on Day Two, we had dropped to fourth. Michael Guest still held top spot in the Subaru—in fact, he'd extended his lead to just over five minutes—while Ross Nicastri had leapt to second outright and Bruce Garland was third. Graeme Wise, in the Pedder's ute, was fifth, while Queensland tyre dealer Mark Griffith had taken his little Toyota RAV4, a vehicle which he and his crew had only completed days before the event, into an amazing sixth position.

This was a brilliant effort by the likable Queenslander. But we all knew that there would be a lot more big efforts needed before the end of this event.

DAY 3

EUCLA
TO
ESPERANCE

DARWIN
Day 10

Katherine

Day 9
Kununurra

Lake
Argyle

Day 8
Curtin
RAAF Base

Daly Waters

Victoria
River

Day 14 Cairns
Day 15 Rest Day

Day 13
Greenvale

Townsville

Day 7
Port Hedland

Day 11
Tennant
Creek

Day 12
Cloncurry

Day 16
Mackay

Hammersley
Range

WA

NT

Alice Springs

QLD

Day 6
Carnarvon

SA

Day 17
Maryborough

Day 5
Geraldton

Flinders
Range

BRISBANE

PERTH

Nullarbor Plain

Lake
Gairdner

Day 2
Eucla

Day 1
Port Augusta

NSW

Great Dividing
Range

Day 18
Coffs Harbour

Day 4
Bunbury

Day 3
Esperance

Bathurst

Day 19

SYDNEY

ADELAIDE
START/FINISH

Day 22

Day 20
Albury

CANBERRA

Day 21
Horsham

VIC

MELBOURNE

TAS

HOBART

How many time zones are there in Australia? Well, in case you don't know, there's at least four—something which many in the cast and crew of the 1998 PlayStation Round Australia Rally discovered thanks to an earlier than expected wake-up call before the start of the third day's run from Eucla to Esperance.

The first vehicle was due to leave Eucla at 5.30 am Western Standard Time (WST). That's the time zone for Perth. But not everyone was aware that there is another time zone— Central Western Standard Time—approximately halfway between Adelaide and Perth. And that's the one which, understandably enough, the hotel wake-up operator at Eucla, which is located just on the Western Australian side of the State border, approximately halfway between Adelaide and Perth, sets her watch to. The zone sits 45 minutes between Perth and Adelaide time.

Most crews had ordered a 4.30 am wake-up call, working on the WST time zone, but instead were roused at 3.45 am. Ouch!

The opening round of battle for the day was a 207 km blast starting just outside Eucla, a perfect way to blow away the cobwebs after not quite enough sleep. The first 150 km of this section ran along the Old Coach Road, the first graded track across this lonely and inhospitable part of the Nullarbor Plain. One can only imagine what it was like when it was a coach track, for even in a modern four-wheel drive, complete with the very latest in suspension, it was a real gut-churner. In a horse-drawn coach it would have been nothing short of a nightmare.

In the 1979 Repco Trial, the dash across the Nullarbor had been one of the deciding stages of the event. Back then, we had to maintain incredible speeds across these car-wrecking roads just to achieve the target times, while the vicious nature of the tracks inevitably led to a rash of punctures.

Vast underground cave systems riddle the limestone plains of the Nullarbor. It's not uncommon to come across one that has fallen in, creating a massive open cavern, which, I'm told, are called 'dolines'. Rally organisers emphasised that we didn't want to get off the track, which was only a single car width; Webby reckoned if you went off into one of those giant craters you'd be able to complete a university course before you hit the bottom.

We started fourth and soon found that the flowing nature of the track, which wound through some fairly open plains, zigging and zagging around limestone outcrops, seemed to suit the Jackaroo. Although we were conceding quite a bit of power to the modified T1 Jackaroos in front of us, not to mention Guest's Subaru rocket, the standard Holden could more than hold its own when the road featured wide, open bends. In the tighter, stop-start stuff our car was at a disadvantage, lacking the grunt to explode out of the corners. We found that the way to get the best from the standard Jackaroo was to maintain the momentum, to stay on the gas and let it flow through the corners.

Still, it came as a major surprise when, only about a third of the way through the stage, we saw the dust plume of Garland's vehicle in front of us, dodging its way across the vast expanse of stunted shrubs and trees. There's nothing quite like being able to see the vehicle in front to get a driver to press on a little harder, and slowly but surely we bridged the gap between Bruce and ourselves until we were sitting in his dust. And, boy, was he making plenty of dust! It washed over the front of our Jack-aroo in waves, at times cutting visibility to almost zero.

It's a bit like trying to drive at 100 km/h down a single-lane road with a shower curtain over the windscreen, and if you can imagine that you can see why I wasn't all that keen to maintain our position.

Thankfully, as I've alluded to, all the competing vehicles were equipped with two-way radios, the plan being that when and if you caught a slower vehicle in a stage, it would be just a case of getting on air and politely requesting to be allowed to pass.

What we didn't know was that inside Garland's stripped-to-the-bone Jackaroo, the noise from the engine and the machine-gun-like sound from the rocks slamming into the floor and guards made it practically impossible to hear anything over the radio. Indeed, the way Bruce describes it, 'It was like a thousand pygmies with little hammers hitting the floor of the car'. He reckoned later that he and his co-driver Harry Suzuki would have been hard pressed to hear a nuclear bomb going off. Before the rally, to reduce the weight of his Jackaroo, Bruce had removed all the sound absorption material. So, despite Webby's increasingly animated pleas over the radio, Bruce just kept on going while I tried to deal with the dust.

At least Webby had the advantage of being able to monitor distances on the trip computer that sat in front of him, so he could still call the major corners. But when a driver can't see the corners, the chances of slipping off the track, even for an instant, increase significantly. More than once I felt we might have clipped a limestone outcrop that lurked by the side of a corner . . .

Suddenly, the Jackaroo suffered a major dose of oversteer, as we slipped and slid all over the countryside. The car was lurching rather dramatically every time we tried to change direction, and I was certain that we'd lost a rear tyre.

Webby undid his belts, popped open his door and quickly confirmed that the tyre had gone. The only thing to do was to stop and change it.

Before the rally started, I said to Webby, 'We're not going to get a flat tyre, it's not happening'. After all, our Bridgestone tyres were kevlar-belted to resist any attack by rocks and were filled with a mousse that would supposedly plug any breech in the defence, should one occur.

'Bewdy!' grinned my navigator.

Now, just three days into the rally, we'd copped a flat.

'Webby,' I asked, 'do you know where the spare wheel and the jack is?'

He just looked blankly at me. This hadn't been in the job description. We were running around like chooks with our heads well and truly cut off.

Webby couldn't believe it. 'Brock,' he said nervously, 'when I get a problem with a car I just ring the manufacturer's PR department.'

Me? As a circuit racer I learnt to rely on my pit crew.

I always say to circuit drivers that the best thing they can do is go in a rally. Rallies teach you a bit of humility, and to put up with all sorts of hardships and bad breaks. Whatever is going down, that's what you've got to contend with. You can't change the conditions, you can't just sit there and delay things to suit yourself. You are just one out of a convoy of 40, 50, maybe 100 cars, and you have to accept that the road surface is going to change, sometimes dramatically change, between the first and last cars. The first driver may fly over a flat, packed surface, but by driver 100 that surface has changed to mud. Alternatively, all the loose stuff might have been thrown off the road by the succession of cars flying through, to leave a much better surface for the later starters. The only certainty is that you can't whinge. You quickly learn to enjoy it and give it your best shot.

Meanwhile, our tyre change was developing into something out of the Keystone Cops. Webby suggested trying to finish the 100 km left in the stage on the shredded tyre, but we both knew that was not an option. Nor was calling the NRMA or the RACV.

Reflecting a false confidence, I left the engine running as we dashed to the rear of the car. But the rear door was locked. Once unlocked, I freed the jack from its cradle just inside the rear door and dived around to start my task of lifting the beast off the ground. While this was happening, however, Webby was discovering that the two spare tyres we carried were secured to the rear floor via a strap that was connected to a ratchet mechanism, and that combination completely dumbfounded him. I was already regretting our failure to actually work out this piece of teamwork beforehand.

Eventually, he got the spare out, after which he went to work with the wheel brace to remove the nuts, with the spare tyre lying next to him on the ground. I was working the jack as hard as I could, sliding under the side of the Jackaroo to ensure that it was placed in the right position. From there, I heard the soft thump of a wheel hitting the ground. The flat was already off, lying next to the spare, which left me precariously located under a couple of tonnes of four-wheel drive with nothing between it and the ground except P. Brock. This was not a situation that made me feel at all comfortable. I've seen too many vehicles fall off the jack over the years to take such a risk, so I strongly urged Webby to get the wheel back on and fasten at least two of the studs. Hey, I was in this event to have some fun, not end up flatter than one of the cardboard Peter Brock cutouts you sometimes see promoting oil at Mobil service stations.

Once the jack had the Jackaroo sufficiently off the ground, the destroyed tyre came off (again!) and the new tyre went on. As soon as a couple of wheel nuts were tight I let it down and started stowing away the jack. The flat went in the rear as well—after all, the rim would be worth big dollars even if the tyre was stuffed—and we both leapt back into the Jackaroo to continue.

This slick bit of teamwork had cost us a mere eight or nine minutes. It seemed like many more. The only positive thing about this sadly ham-fisted effort was that, despite the length of our unscheduled stop, not another vehicle had passed us, which led us to believe that we had established a significant jump on those pursuing us.

And then, too quickly, just a little further down the track, we started hitting dust again. But it didn't smell like dust, more like burning oil or rubber. Someone was in trouble. At first we thought it must have been Bruce Garland, his being the vehicle immediately in front of us in the field. Hey, we thought, if we could have a flat, why not Bruce? Maybe he had decided to soldier on.

However, when we crested a small rise, we saw instead the Subaru of Michael Guest, limping along at almost no speed with what appeared to be massive damage. We discovered later that Michael had tried to straight-line a corner at high speed only to discover that the long grass hid a rock only slightly smaller that Uluru. We had seen a rock, now lying in the middle of the road, a few kilometres back up the trail, but initially dismissed it. After all, finding a big rock in the middle of a rough track is not at all unusual.

What the offending boulder had done was rip the guts from the low-slung Subaru, turning a potent and potentially rally-winning weapon into a lame duck that would need a miracle to reach the end of the stage without incurring massive penalties. Guest, effectively, was out of contention; he tried to drive the remaining 100 km with a smashed rear suspension and brake caliper, and one punctured tyre (he'd punctured one left-hand tyre, then both right-hand tyres and only had two spares) but became stuck around 26 km from the finish. His costly mishap confirmed what we believed all along—that in the outback, the tougher the going got, the better the big 4 × 4 brigade would like it—and reinforced our pre-race strategy. If we could build enough of a buffer in the truly daunting conditions of the first half of the rally, that time might make up for what we believed would be our lack of nimbleness and speed when the event hit the smoother, faster roads down the east coast.

Herein lies the trick to long-distance competition—you have to be alive at the end of the event to have any chance of winning it. Sounds obvious, but how many times have you seen guys go at breakneck speed at the start of the Bathurst race only to be missing in action when it all gets down to the business end of proceedings? I've won at Bathurst when I haven't had the fastest car. It's all about playing with the cards you've been dealt, of making the most of what you've got and turning what you do have to your advantage.

All you can ever do is to go with your gut feeling as to how fast the car can go. If you go faster than that, and your judgment's correct, then the car will fall apart; go slower and you'll fall off the pace. Consequently, to be successful you need to be in tune with the car and the conditions. A lot of this you get from experience, from learning from previous stages and previous rallies.

The conditions from Eucla to Esperance were extremely rough, the most demanding of the rally to date, and that's what caught Michael Guest out. We lost 14 minutes ourselves, but bar for the time sacrificed changing tyres, we couldn't have gone any faster. We were obliged to lose some seconds on this rough stuff. Against the other two modified Jackaroos ahead of us, our car needed specially welded-up heavy-duty suspension to be competitive without potentially being wrecked. As it was, at one point I bent a front wishbone and drove for a long time late in the day with my steering wheel up between my knees.

This was the first time anything had happened to the car at all, and I feared the worst. However, when we reached the end of the stage, we found that our crew merely had to replace one part. It was reassuring to know that the car wasn't found wanting during this stage, just one component of it.

I was more than happy with our efforts on the day. Without the flat I reckon we could have been in the lead, but we were still running a strong third, trailing only the other Jackaroos of Ross Nicastri and Bruce Garland. Apart from Guesty's Subaru, the other major casualty of the day was John Anderson, who had been airlifted to Kalgoorlie Hospital with his arm broken in four places after rolling his Peugeot on the Nullarbor.

The drive into Esperance was typical of our experiences in the towns the PlayStation visited. Quite seriously, we'd drive into what at first glance would appear to be a ghost town. But then we'd arrive at the local showground to be met by many hundreds, sometimes thousands, of people. For the citizens of these locations, this is a huge event, a major national sporting adventure visiting *their* town. I'd be chaperoned towards queues of fans waiting for autographs and photos, after which I'd complete interviews with the local newspapers, TV and radio.

Day Three was a reminder of the role of luck in endurance rallies. That flat had cost us time we would struggle to make up for the rest of the event. It reminded me of a story Bruce Garland told of an experience he had in 1995, when he was up with the leaders in his Jackaroo. Unfortunately, perhaps because he was a tad fatigued, he rolled the car. Fortunately, the vehicle rolled back onto its wheels, and the whole incident only cost Bruce 30 seconds or so.

However, if he'd rolled the car onto its side, they might have lost 15 to 20 minutes waiting for assistance. As Bruce puts it, 'Who knows what'll happen out there. It's the old story of Murphy's Law . . .

'Sometimes it works against you, sometimes for you.'

DAY 4

ESPERANCE
TO
BUNBURY

D ay Four should have provided a great day's competition, but by the time we started there were just two 24 km stages to negotiate. It appeared that bureaucratic red tape from local governments had left the organisers with no option but to ditch three stages, leaving the field with less than 50 km of no-holds-barred action during a day that would see the rally trek over 800 km to the next stop of Bunbury.

The now-resuscitated Subaru that had been driven at breakneck speed by rally ace Michael Guest was continuing in the event, even though it had no chance of victory. It also had a new head driver, with Guest having flown home, leaving the driving duties to his co-driver Jason Walk and a third man, Paul Pyyvaara.

'There's no chance we can win the event from here,' Guest had told reporters before departing. 'I was only here for one reason ... to win. The best thing that can happen now is for the two younger members of the team to go on and get more rallying experience.'

Leading up to the PlayStation, Michael Guest was regarded by the press as a warm favourite, on the back of his impressive performances in a number of much shorter rallies. In fact, he'd caught the eye of several judges in Europe and later had a good drive in the world rally championship.

But, at least in the eyes of the off-road drivers in this event, Guesty wasn't favourite. They considered the marriage of his ultra-aggressive style and the relatively low-bodied Subaru would be a dangerous one on tracks on the Nullarbor and in Western Australia, which we considered would suit the Jackaroos. I even predicted to the media, after Day Two, that his car would break in the rough stuff if he tried to go too fast.

How do I compare with someone such as Guesty? Well, I am not a rally driver nor an off-roader. I am a race driver who has driven in a few rallies and in off-road endurance events. I've reached the point where neither rallies nor off-road fazes me. I don't care if it is a wet road at Bathurst or a shocking piece of corrugated stuff in the outback of Australia. It is just a piece of road and I've got to adapt to it, so I can drive down quickly, as quickly as I can. And the key to adapting effectively is developing a rapport with the car and the conditions, and knowing the limits of both.

Part of the challenge of a round-Australia event is not knowing where the next corner might be, or where the road is going. The sheer vastness of the event makes it logistically impossible for drivers to be made aware of every last rock and pothole and mud patch bend in the road. By contrast, drivers in World Rally Championship events, even State and Australian Championships, get to practise on the rally tracks in much the same way drivers rehearse on Mount Panorama at Bathurst.

The generosity of Holden dealers around the nation during the PlayStation was remarkable. Not only did they provide servicing facilities, but on occasions they threw a barbecue for the team, the proceeds helping Bruce Garland balance his budget for the three-week event. Some people might have got the impression that we had money to burn, but in reality the finances were tight. Bruce was doing an amazing job putting such a professional show on the road for the kind of money that some manufacturers would spend on corporate hospitality at Bathurst.

Helping to keep the coffers topped up was Garland's

booming little merchandise business run by Ed Mulligan. It was up to Ed to run in front of the team and set up at each town along the rally route, ready to sell T-shirts, hats and other rally and Brock merchandise to the eager locals. Bruce and Ed, ever the entrepreneurs, even had replicas of the Brock number plates that appeared on the 05 Jackaroo made up. While this was hardly an enterprise to rival some of the world's giant corporations, it did earn enough to keep the team fed. In fact, Bruce kept joking to us that he needed it to sustain his cash flow to ensure he and his team would be able to get to the next town.

Or was he joking?

Despite having only two stages to complete during the day, at least they were both great fun—fast, challenging and with a few nasty stings that could hurt those who didn't keep their mind on the job.

The second, run to the north-east of Ravensthorpe alongside the side of Mt Benson, was typical Western Australian rally country. The surface was loose, ball-bearing gravel, the kind of road where two-wheel drive cars struggle for traction. Indeed, it's like driving on marbles—superb fun but a potentially huge moment is always lurking.

About 17.5 km into the stage, after blazing up a very steep climb, we came to a crest. Where the road turned left, there stood a sign. Here we were, in the middle of nowhere at the top of an escarpment, and someone with an evil sense of humour had placed a 'Rail-Xing' sign that no doubt had confounded tourists for years. Not to be fooled, we ploughed on, confident that, given there were actually no railway tracks, it was highly unlikely that a train would suddenly appear.

By around 9.30 am we had the stage finished, and that was basically it for the day. After a quick service at Ravensthorpe, a little village of just over 300 people, there was nothing left for the day but a 580 km transport stage up the highway to Bunbury, where we would bed down for the night.

The countryside around Ravensthorpe is a real eye-opener, some of the most beautiful countryside you'll see anywhere in Australia. Beautiful lush pastures, rolling fields, a lot of very healthy-looking crops, with wooded mountains popping up every so often. This part of Western Australia is totally different to the rest of the State, looking much more like the Otway Ranges in south-west Victoria. I know I'm beginning to sound like a tourist brochure but I, like I'm sure many others, have always had a mental picture of Western Australia as sand and desert and tough country, but this is very fertile land.

After we'd parked the Jackaroo for the night, I met up with Bruce Garland. Having prepared my car for the race he knew it at least as well as I did. Because of the modifications he'd done to his car, he knew it was just about unbreakable. He knew, too, that while it was ultra-tough, mine wasn't quite so indestructible.

'Brockie,' he was warning me again, 'your credit meter started ticking the first day you hit a pothole.'

'It's all right, Bruce,' I assured him, 'don't worry.'

'Tick, tick, tick,' he continued. 'You went a bit quick today, didn't you? Only so many credits, you know Brockie, and then you're gone.'

And then he climbed under the car, just to have a look. I think his great ambition was that, when we finally made it back to Adelaide, his cars would finish in first and second place.

The emphasis on reliability is, for me, one of the great attractions of this type of event. No one wanted to see a scenario where cars were pushed to their limit by day and then rejuvenated every night. With the right crew and right sized budget it's possible to rebuild a fragile but super-quick hot rod overnight, to just throw the broken bits away and put new replacements in. But organisers wanted vehicles to be tested to the limit. They also wanted drivers to be aware that if they were a little bit clumsy and didn't show any regard for the machinery they were going to pay for it. So they introduced regulations such as limited service time, and not allowing anyone other than the driver or co-driver to work on vehicles during transport or competitive stages. In fact, the rules were so stringent that service crews weren't even allowed to provide food or drink for their drivers while the race was going on.

However, when the crews did have access to the cars, the camaraderie of rallying would often come to the fore. For example, Bruce Garland's team was responsible for the welfare of two cars, Bruce's and mine. But there were other cars in the rally that he had built, or been involved with in some way, and inevitably the drivers of those cars would come up to him and ask, 'Bruce, we've got a problem, have you got a spare?'

And, of course, he would say, 'Here's what you're after.'

Or he might say, 'Mate, if we use this up now I am going to need another spare for Brockie's car by the time we get down the road. What I need you to do is to ring up Melbourne or Sydney and get them to get the part on a plane ...'

The way these guys all work together is amazing. There's a lot of very clever, very straight-up-and-down people involved in off-road endurance rallying. For some who don't know the sport, it's very easy to dismiss these blokes as a bunch of cowboys who belt around in the sticks without any idea of what is going on. That's dead wrong. These fellas are savvy.

And they love a challenge.

DAY 5

BUNBURY
TO
GERALDTON

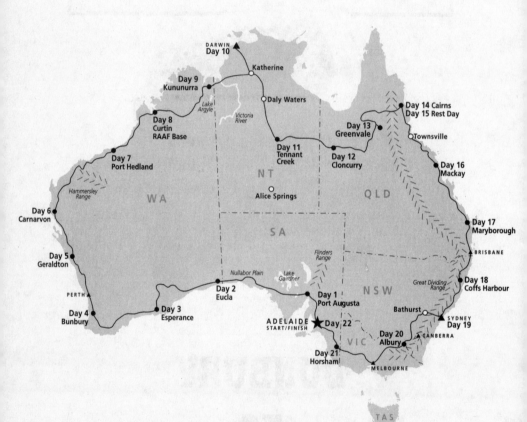

DARWIN
Day 10

Day 9
Kununurra

Lake
Argyle

Victoria
River

Katherine

Daly Waters

Day 8
Curtin
RAAF Base

Day 11
Tennant
Creek

Day 12
Cloncurry

Day 13
Greenvale

Day 14 Cairns
Day 15 Rest Day

Townsville

Day 7
Port Hedland

Hammersley
Range

N T

Alice Springs

Q L D

Day 16
Mackay

W A

Day 6
Carnarvon

S A

Day 17
Maryborough

BRISBANE

Day 5
Geraldton

Flinders
Range

Nullabor Plain

Lake
Gairdner

Great Dividing
Range

Day 18
Coffs Harbour

PERTH

Day 2
Eucla

Day 1
Port Augusta

N S W

Bathurst

SYDNEY
Day 19

Day 4
Bunbury

Day 3
Esperance

ADELAIDE
START/FINISH

Day 22

Day 20
Albury

CANBERRA

Day 21
Horsham

V I C

MELBOURNE

T A S

HOBART

With Michael Guest's Subaru no longer in contention, and with the special stages becoming increasingly demanding, the big four-wheel drives were edging away from the car brigade who had to take it easy over the rough stuff to prevent potentially mortal mechanical damage.

The first hit-out of Day Five began near Serpentine Dam, south-east of Perth. The course had previously been used during the World Rally Championship round which Western Australia hosts with such amazing success each year, and in a number of local rally events. Everyone concurred afterwards that it was a magnificent driver's stage. It featured a range of tracks, from fast, ball-bearing gravel roads to pathways that were in reality little more than a couple of sandy wheel tracks. With the tight, twisting terrain, any mistake would almost surely mean hitting something. And something meant a tree.

At just under 33 km long, this stage was a nice warm-up for the day, which saw the field put another 835 km under the wheels as they headed up the Western Australian coast.

The second stage of the day was held out near Wanneroo, home of Perth's only major motor racing circuit. The track used to be called Wanneroo Park, but since it was purchased by wealthy Western Australian car dealer Alf Barbargello, it has been renamed, rather obviously, Barbargello Raceway. This is where the V8 touring cars come each year for the Western Australian round of the Australian Touring Car Championship and it's a very challenging and demanding circuit.

I remember racing at Wanneroo—or Barbargello if you like—for the first time back in 1971. In fact, during the 1998

PlayStation we even drove past the BP service station on the corner of Wanneroo Rd, which I had to visit on that race day in 1971 to pick up something or other to fix my car. I remember leaping into a road car, blasting out of the circuit and getting to the servo only to find myself confronted by the traffic jam from hell when I tried to get back to the track.

It looked like just about everyone in Perth was heading out to the track for a day at the races, and with time ticking away before the start of my race, I was facing the very real possibility of not making it back in time for the start. Anxiety building, I flagged down a police car, explained the situation, and the boys in blue did the rest. Even though it was the very beginning of my career, that incident remains the first and only time I've ever arrived at a circuit with a full police escort leading me to the track with sirens wailing and lights flashing.

Another memory of Wanneroo ... back in 1979, we arrived at the Wanneroo circuit for a bitumen stage of the Repco Round Australia Trial. At that point in the rally my old Holden Dealer Team colleague, Colin Bond, was making his presence felt in his Ford Cortina. He was up with the leaders when he left the circuit, but only a few kilometres down the road he missed a corner and rolled into a paddock. Eventually the team got the battered Cortina back on its wheels and back on the road, but the car had suffered the kind of damage that meant it was no longer a contender for outright honours in the trial. It's that easy to lose a gruelling test such as a round-Australia ... just one mistake and it can all be over.

The second stage of the day looked right up our alley—a fast, flowing 66 km dash around the perimeter of a pine plantation where we could build up some speed and let the Jackaroo off its leash. This was an absolutely brilliant piece of road, smooth and very fast, with crests punctuating some very long straights where the Jackaroo could get a little air time. At one point, we were absolutely rocketing along, the Jackaroo handling the conditions in sensational style, when we crested a rise at warp speed only to discover that the road dropped away more suddenly than we'd anticipated.

I don't think I've ever been in a vehicle that has spent so long in the air; in fact we were up so high for so long that we had time to look at each other and discuss our imminent return to earth. Much longer in the air and I reckon I would have had to apply for a pilot's licence. Eventually the Jackaroo came back to earth, just a little awkwardly, landing on the right front wheel and hitting the bump stops on the suspension before settling down.

Soon after, we arrived at a T-intersection at the top of a rise where we had to turn hard left. Admittedly, I left my braking to what I thought was the last possible moment—but I soon realised I was past the 'last possible moment' and into the 'oh, it's a little too late' category. From the wheel tracks that lay in front of us, it seemed that the vehicles of the leaders, Nicastri and Garland, had done the same thing. There was clear evidence that two cars had speared across the road before performing U-turns in the soft, sandy sidetrack on the other side of the road.

And that's exactly what we should have done, but no sooner had we entered the escape road and started our U-turn when the Jackaroo just ground to a halt. We were bogged big-time. Sure, the sand was deep, but nothing that should stop the progress of a four-wheel drive ... yet it had.

I assumed we weren't in four-wheel drive, but the lever *was* in the right position, so I grabbed low-range four-wheel drive and dropped the clutch. But we just sank deeper into the sand. Maybe the front hubs weren't locked in, I suggested.

Webby dived out from the passenger side to check while I shifted into high-range four-wheel drive and gave it a big dose of revs, and yet again let out the clutch. Still, we didn't move. Well, we did move, but unfortunately, we were going downwards rather than forwards, the rear tyres sinking the vehicle ever deeper and deeper into trouble.

I leapt from the driver's seat to look underneath, and found that we weren't just stuck in the sand, we'd basically commenced our own mining operation. The rear diff was all but buried; the Jackaroo sat stranded. I started trying to clear away the sand, while Webby began grabbing at branches and rocks to put under the wheels.

It was now clear to me that the reason we had become so comprehensively trapped was that while it appeared from the driver's seat that we were in four-wheel drive, we had careered off the road in two-wheel drive and were now stuck in two-wheel drive. Thus, we couldn't escape without either a tow or an airlift. Webby was dispatched to the rear of the Jackaroo to find the snatch strap we had just in case of such dire circumstances, while I went to the middle of the road to flag down some help.

On a number of occasions during the rally, I took the Jackaroo out of four-wheel drive and put it into two-wheel drive, because in my view four-wheel drive is of no advantage in certain driving conditions. This was something I learnt as I went along. If we encountered twisty, gravelly tracks, for example, I might lean towards two-wheel drive. I found I could sometimes place the car into a corner very well in two-wheel drive. The car would go very, very sideways, and I loved it. You could almost go backwards down the road.

My use of two-wheel drive also reflected the dilemma we were facing. I couldn't go that hard over the really rough stuff because my car wasn't modified to suit those conditions, so the only time I could make up any time on my chief rivals was in the flatter, smoother terrain that also suited them. But there was one type of road where I could grab some time— the undulating twisty roads, which I often attacked in two-wheel drive to enhance this slight advantage. Some cars hated the rough stuff where there was little or no clearance between the road and the chassis. Other vehicles didn't like the flat stuff because they lacked outright speed. My Jackaroo, in contrast, was a nice all-rounder, never dominant but never deficient either.

Frustratingly, our fellow competitors did start arriving ... and leaving without stopping to help. Because the turn was right on a crest, they couldn't see us while they were turning and thus missed my impressive and impassioned impersonation of a windmill. Car after car roared by, with me yelling and screaming and, at one stage, even running up the road with arms waving like a drowning man trying to get some attention.

Finally, the big Nissan Patrol of Reg Owen came into view, started to turn and then ground to a halt. I can't stress how delighted I was to see his gleaming reversing lights come on, as he backed up to where we were stranded. His navigator, Russell Cairns, jumped out to attach our tow rope to the rear of the Nissan, and with one mighty tug the Jackaroo popped out of the sand like a cork from a bottle. After 15 minutes of crazed inactivity, we were back on the track and in business.

We hurtled off towards the end of the stage, passing Owen and then hauling in another couple of slower vehicles. However, it soon became clear that we weren't out of the woods— literally and metaphorically speaking—just yet. We were nearing the edge of the stage when the most almighty grinding sound started to come from the front of the Jackaroo. It was the kind of sickening mechanical noise that every driver dreads—the crunching, tearing, ripping echo of metal on metal.

So there was no option but to revert to a cautious limp to the end of the stage, leap on the radio to alert the service crew and nurse the Jackaroo down the road to help, which thankfully was a mere 12 km away.

As soon as we pulled up, the boys were under the Jackaroo to survey the damage. From experience they knew exactly where to look. The front right drive shaft had snapped. This, we discovered, was a problem Bruce Garland had solved in his vehicle by manufacturing indestructible front drive shafts in his own workshop. But since we were running a standard vehicle we were equipped with standard components.

With only 20 minutes available to them, the guys had no time to replace the shaft; the job requires pulling out the whole front end. So they simply removed the broken part— a job that took the best part of three minutes—and informed us that, for the rest of the day at least, we'd have the only two-wheel drive Jackaroo in the country. A minor problem, but we were still running.

And with only one more stage left to run before the stop in Geraldton, what could have been a disaster became nothing really more than a minor, if hugely frustrating, setback.

Funnily enough, on that final stage, a 17 km run over a very fast shire road, we were the quickest vehicle. During the stage, I saw the fastest speed yet on the speedo: 175 km/h. Maybe we should have been in two-wheel drive from the start!

But even being quick on the final leg couldn't overcome the damage that our time playing in the sand had caused. Our position for the day was 27th, though we were still third outright. However, because the field regrouped each morning based on the finishing positions from the day before, we'd be starting tomorrow a lot later than normal, and be obliged to work our way through a host of slower cars and contend with the inevitable dust.

Why then, did that part on the Jackaroo break? Because, I was told afterwards, when we made that huge long jump prior to our unscheduled stop in the bunker, I kept my foot on the accelerator. Under these circumstances, in four-wheel drive, the front wheels drop down, leaving one or both of the front half shafts and the front axle hanging down. The car's not built to work at that angle, and stresses are created that can cause the most susceptible of the front half shafts to crack, and then snap when the car finally lands. In this instance, with the right front half shaft gone, we were left in two-wheel drive and without the power to get out of the sand. Of course, Webby and I had not been aware we'd smashed the drive shaft until we were stuck in the sand, wondering where the four-wheel drive had gone.

All I needed to do to avoid putting unnecessary pressure on the drive shafts again was keep my foot off the power when we were in mid-air. That would take the pressure off the front of the car. Simple really.

Another lesson learned.

DAY 6

GERALDTON
TO
CARNARVON

DARWIN
Day 10 ▲

Katherine ●

Day 9
Kununurra ●

○ Daly Waters

● Day 14 Cairns
Day 15 Rest Day

○ Townsville

Day 8
Curtin
RAAF Base ●

*Lake
Argyle*

*Victoria
River*

Day 13
Greenvale ●

Day 7
Port Hedland ●

Day 11
Tennant
Creek ●

Day 12
Cloncurry ●

Day 16
Mackay ●

N T

*Hammersley
Range*

○ Alice Springs

W A

Q L D

Day 6
Carnarvon ●

Day 17
Maryborough ●

S A

▲ BRISBANE

*Flinders
Range*

Day 5
Geraldton ●

Nullabor Plain

*Lake
Gairdner*

N S W

*Great Dividing
Range*

Day 18
Coffs Harbour ●

PERTH ●

Day 2
Eucla ●

Day 1
Port Augusta ●

Bathurst ●

Day 4
Bunbury ●

Day 3
Esperance ●

A D E L A I D E
START/FINISH ★ **Day 22**

▲ SYDNEY
Day 19

▲ CANBERRA

V I C

Day 20
Albury ●

Day 21
Horsham ●

▲ MELBOURNE

T A S

▲ HOBART

Although the 1998 PlayStation Round Australia didn't travel to Tasmania, the Apple Isle still had a significant role in the event, by contributing the safety team that accompanied the rally around the country.

Heading the team was Geoff Becker, who in real life is the chief safety officer for the ambulance service in Burnie. Other members of the safety team, all with experience garnered from previous major endurance rallies including the 1995 round-Australia and Targa Tasmania, came from other parts of Tassie, including Devonport, Smithton and Hobart. Featuring experts in rally trauma and rescue, the team included specialist fire suppression, patient extrication and accident investigation personnel.

The fleet of vehicles that carried the safety team comprised three Toyota LandCruiser Troop-carriers which had been fitted out to ambulance configuration, three Hilux utilities with canopies, to be used as first intervention and rescue vehicles, plus a LandCruiser from which Becker could oversee the proceedings.

The safety team members were sourced through Motor Sport Safety and Rescue, an organisation that supplies staff and services to many rallies throughout eastern Australia. For the 1998 PlayStation Round Australia, they worked closely with State and territory ambulance services, and the Royal Flying Doctor Service.

No driver, no matter how good, can ever expect to win a motor race without a top-class crew, and I have to say that the guys that Bruce Garland assembled for the PlayStation Rally are among the best I've ever worked with.

No fuss, no bother, no whingeing or whining, they just got on with the job. Their speed and efficiency was a credit to their professionalism and dedication to getting the job done, ensuring that the two Jackaroos were always in the best condition possible.

From the moment we rolled into the overnight stopping point at Geraldton they were on the job, tearing out the front end of the Jackaroo and bolting in a new one. By the time we arrived in the early morning for the start of the sixth day of adventure, car No 05 was back in mechanically pristine condition.

I mention this because, all too often, it's the driver who gets all the credit while the crew is forgotten. But I can tell you, none of my Bathurst victories would have been achieved without having a dedicated bunch of guys handling the mechanical side of the business.

As we rolled out of Geraldton, I was fully aware that, from a starting position of 27th, this day was going to be long, hot and dusty. If you lose, say, 15 minutes on one day, you're going to lose a bit more time on the following day because of the seconds you lose getting past the slower cars. The trick would be to go as hard as possible so that, when the field was re-seeded at the end of the day, we'd be back in the leading bunch.

In front of us there were a lot of other competitors, all trying to do their best, so we'd have our work cut out for us. However, with six stages to complete during the day, the longest being 114 km, time was on our side.

The first stage of Day Six was just under 20 km long, so with the competitors leaving at one-minute intervals, we really couldn't make all that much of an impact on those in front of us. To make matters even more difficult, we were caught briefly in the dust of one of the rapid-response medical intervention vehicles spread throughout the field.

This may sound annoying, but in an event with some incredibly long stages, it's actually reassuring to know that if the worst does happen, medical attention can be on the spot in minutes rather than hours—for this can literally mean the difference between life and death. Geoff Becker had assembled a highly-qualified and dedicated crew of paramedics and doctors to follow the event. They were spread throughout the field, driving through the special stages in vehicles supplied by Toyota.

Becker has been involved with motorsport for years and truly has the best interests of the competitors at heart—well, most of the time, anyway.

He also has an evil sense of humour and doesn't mind the occasional practical joke. On Day Five, he'd pulled one of the best I've ever seen on Bruce Garland. It was, indeed, a real jewel of a 'gotcha'.

Bruce, you see, has a habit of being the practical joker rather than the 'jokee'. This fact, I'm sure, no doubt inspired Geoff to come up with his crowning moment.

We were preparing for the first special stage after leaving Perth, the fateful second stage of the day when we damaged the drive shaft. Geoff sidled up to me and whispered, 'Brockie, how you goin'?'

'Not too bad, mate, not too bad at all,' I replied.

'Well come with me, I want to have some fun. I'm going to give Garland a drug test.'

'A what?'

'A drug test, I'm going to give Bruce a random drug test.'

This I had to see. And I made sure the cameras were ready.

With a straight face, not even a hint of mirth, Geoff strode over to Bruce's Jackaroo and informed him that, according to the regulations of the world governing body of motorsport (FIA), and also on the advice of CAMS and the Australian Institute of Sport, random drug tests had to be carried out. 'Unfortunately, Bruce, your name's come out of the hat,' Geoff explained.

We're talking only minutes before the start of a special stage here. Before he donned his driver's helmet, Bruce had to submit to a blood test. In Geoff's right hand was the needle required for the job. And this was no ordinary needle, this was a dirty big spear gun.

'Oh, bull,' was Bruce's response.

'Sorry, Bruce, rules are rules,' the doctor was insistent. 'A bit of blood won't hurt.' At this point, the ever-expanding crowd got involved, suggesting Bruce shouldn't be a wimp, that he was scared of needles, and so on.

'Clench your fist, c'mon, I've got to find a vein.' Geoff was having a ball.

'My God!' roared Bruce Garland, 'I can't believe you're doing this. Me? Drugs?'

The sight of that needle and the thought of having to spill blood turned Bruce's face pale. He maintained rather loudly that this was a 'setup'. They couldn't possibly be serious. Geoff Becker, though, maintained a straight face and started to roll up Bruce's sleeve, at the same time recalling a variety of FIA regulation numbers and explanations. Next came a tourniquet ... in fact, it wasn't until the needle was poised over the protruding vein that our Chief Safety Officer cried, 'Gotcha!' and erupted in uncontrolled laughter. Bruce didn't know whether to be angry, relieved or just join in the joke, while the rest of us rolled around and enjoyed our fellow competitor's discomfort.

He surprised us a bit with this prank, did Geoff Becker. Impressed us, too.

It wasn't until we had completed the first two special stages of Day Six that we discovered that our front hubs were unlocked, which meant that we were actually in two-wheel drive, rather than the four-wheel drive we wanted to be in. Luckily this oversight, and that's all it turned out to be, didn't create any dramas—I just pretended I was driving a Commodore. However Webby and I made a mental note to ensure that the state of the hubs was one of the first things checked each and every morning.

Each of the Jackaroo's front hubs has a switch which, when locked in, engages the front wheels to drive the vehicle when the driver selects four-wheel drive. If these switches are not locked in, the car drives like a conventional two-wheel drive vehicle, even if the driver has selected four-wheel drive. Some four-wheel drives have an electronic switch on the dashboard to allow the driver to lock in the hubs without leaving the driver's seat, but with the Jackaroo you have to climb out of the vehicle and lock the hubs in.

Before the day's racing began, I assumed that the hubs had been locked in. Because the car had a brand new diff and various other new components, we'd decided it would be sensible to work the engine back up to full pace gradually, so we gave it a bit of a run over. So, when we left Geraldton, I assumed the crew had locked the hubs in, but I didn't select four-wheel drive straight away, to give the car a chance to turn itself over. But when I got up the road a distance, I selected four-wheel drive . . . and it wasn't working. So I got on the two-way radio, and the boys moaned, 'Oh no, it's broken again'.

But I didn't think it was. It just felt weird. We ran with great trepidation there for the first half of the day, pressing on in two-wheel drive. I was contemplating the rest of the journey around Australia in two-wheel drive until we finally realised that the front hubs weren't locked in.

'Didn't you guys do it?' I asked the crew.

'We thought you did,' they replied.

Later, we discovered that one of the guys had locked them in for us but then someone else, aware that we wanted to just turn the engine over on the transport stage out of town, came along and unlocked them. The thing is, they forgot that I was a totally new boy at this four-wheel drive caper. I really hadn't got stuck into how these four-wheel drives work; hadn't learned that some 4 × 4s have electronic locking, others have optional electronic locking, while some you need to get out there and do it manually. I assumed you just turn the car on and go, but there are a lot of little intricacies—in essence, this event was a crash course for me in the art of four-wheel drives. The guys in the crew thought, 'Peter Brock, yeah, he knows about all these things'.

Take it from me, he doesn't!

The track on which the first special stage of Day Six was run skirted some huge wheat fields. The new crop stood around waist high and the owners, obviously keen to enjoy a bountiful harvest, asked that the competitors stay on the road and out of their crop. This, of course, was a highly reasonable request, but on one tight corner I got it all crossed up and went spearing off the track, carving a rather distinctive swathe through the field in the process.

Aside from this slight mishap, and the dust of our competitors, one of the major hazards this day was emus. They were out in big numbers and a tad too stupid to see the sense in staying away from the rally cars racing through the countryside.

These birds have zero road sense. And good speed, capable of getting up to around 60 km/h. Out here the locals call them 'bush chooks'. But such a description doesn't give a good indication of their size. Take it from me, a fully-grown emu is not the kind of thing you want to hit at speed. Aside from making a mess of the emu, a collision would make a huge dent in even the most sturdy of vehicles. And, because they stand so tall on their gangly legs, it's very possible that after smashing into the front of the vehicle, the bird can often roll up the bonnet and through the windscreen. People who have had this happen to their car tell me that having a seriously injured emu in the passenger compartment, its legs kicking and feathers flying, is not particularly pleasant and is downright dangerous. It's not something I want to experience first-hand.

During the final stage of the day, we stopped briefly as we passed the homestead of the station which the stage ran through. This one property on the Western Australian coast covered roughly half a million hectares. There are smaller countries than that!

What occurred at the homestead was similar to what would happen on numerous occasions during the event, and typifies for me a part of the spirit of the bush.

When you approach a homestead you find they are all there, in or on their cars and utes, leaning on tractors or the station's plane, hanging off fence posts, or staying cautiously back on the homestead balconies to see the rally go through. By 'they' I mean the owners and their families, and the station workers, including the shearers, the jackaroos and the jillaroos. Some are usually planning to head out to a nearby corner—of course, they know which corners to go to—to get the best possible view of the action.

They'll ask, 'Which way you goin'?' And after you've pointed, perhaps, in a north-westerly direction, they'll continue, 'Headin' out that way. How long before you're leavin'?'

'Twenty minutes,' you reply.

'We'll head up there, about 3 km up the road . . . there's a big left-hander.'

Now you're excited. 'I'll look out for you,' you might reply. 'Don't worry, I'll chuck it sideways.'

And you do! As far as all are concerned, it's worth it. They've had some fun, you've had some fun.

There are photos to be taken and autographs to be signed. Inevitably, you'll be invited back, meanwhile you're wishing there was more time before you have to drive off.

Some are from the UK or Europe, out for a spot of jackaroo and jillaroo work. Many are in their twenties, having finished their schooling and seeking to broaden their horizons before they decide exactly what they're going to do for a career. And, of course, there are young adults from Australia's big cities who are doing exactly the same thing.

It's genuinely great to talk to them. Many, from different generations, have spent time in the city, at uni, in business suits, in various trades, but have learnt through such experiences that life in the bush is the way to go for them.

This is one of the advantages of being the 'celebrity' driver in a round-Australia. A vast array of extremely generous and interesting people want to meet and talk to you. Mum might have especially cooked you some scones. 'Wanna cuppa?' a kind soul will invariably ask. These people are very strong, tough, resilient. They admire what we do on the road—'Gee, we wouldn't want to be driving on *those* tracks,' they'll laugh—but also see it as being pretty frivolous. Like a rodeo, just a bit of fun, some time off from everyday life.

A number of station owners fly their own planes. Some

would take off just before we began a stage so they could check out the rally from the air. I remember one very funny situation. We had made a wrong decision, taking the wrong road when we arrived at a fork. By the time we got back on the right track we were stuck behind a slower car. Over the two-way, Webby asked if we could pass, but this was the driver in front's big moment and he refused to immediately let us through. Suddenly, over the two-way, came a booming voice from above: 'Listen pal, Brockie's right behind you, so *move over*'. It was coming from the pilot of a plane overhead, but to the offending driver, it must have sounded like God.

In next to no time, we were through.

Back to Day Six. Into the final stage, and we'd managed to have a completely trouble-free day.

But then, we found ourselves on a track that took us alongside the edge of Shark Bay. The surface was slippery and the track was lined with trees. In an effort to straight-line the corners as much as possible, and keep the speed up, I was clipping the branches of the overhanging foliage. This wasn't a problem, at least not until I clipped something decidedly more solid than leaves. I reckon that we hit whatever it was at roughly 160 km/h, and the windscreen on my side of the vehicle shattered under the force of the impact.

Carnarvon's local Windscreens O'Brien representative was actually waiting for us when we rolled into our overnight resting point. It had been a tough but highly enjoyable day, really tough in fact, as we raced our way past the slower cars that had begun in front of us. But we had been fast enough to finish second on the day and move into second place outright. Bruce was now in the lead, as Ross Nicastri had some major problems. Ross had suddenly found that his Jackaroo was running on just five cylinders. He reckoned that dirt had got into the fuel system and blown a piston, though I wondered if he'd tuned his engine to the point that it was running a little bit lean at certain revs. Whatever, Ross would press on, after having new engine parts road-freighted up to Carnarvon, but his chances of winning outright had gone.

More good news came for Bruce later in the evening when at an AMP (one of the major sponsors of the round-Australia) function, the windscreen I had smashed, and then signed, raised an astounding $450 for a local charity. Bruce immediately saw the value in the three spare windscreens he had in his parts truck and seriously contemplated hitting them all with a hammer to help top up his budget.

I think he was joking, but ...

DAY 7

CARNARVON
TO
PORT HEDLAND

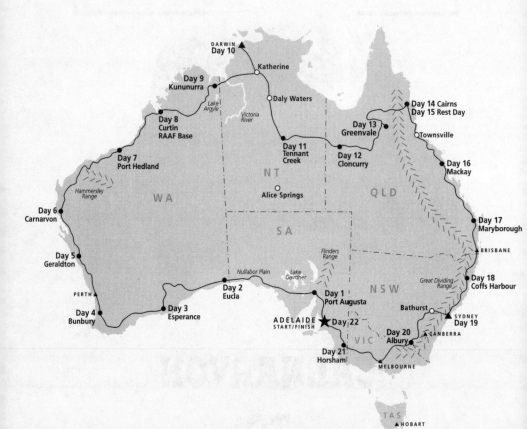

DARWIN
Day 10

Katherine

Day 9
Kununurra

Lake
Argyle

Day 8
Curtin
RAAF Base

Victoria
River

Daly Waters

Day 14 Cairns
Day 15 Rest Day

Day 13
Greenvale

Townsville

Day 7
Port Hedland

Day 11
Tennant
Creek

Day 12
Cloncurry

Day 16
Mackay

Hammersley
Range

N T

Day 17
Maryborough

Alice Springs

W A

Q L D

Day 6
Carnarvon

S A

BRISBANE

Day 5
Geraldton

Flinders
Range

Nullarbor Plain

Lake
Gairdner

Great Dividing
Range

Day 18
Coffs Harbour

PERTH

N S W

Bathurst

Day 2
Eucla

Day 1
Port Augusta

Day 4
Bunbury

Day 3
Esperance

SYDNEY

Day 19

ADELAIDE
START/FINISH

Day 22

CANBERRA

Day 20
Albury

V I C

Day 21
Horsham

MELBOURNE

T A S

HOBART

D ay Seven would be one of the longest driving days of the PlayStation rally—an energy-sapping, concentration-testing 1100 km run up the Western Australian coast.

A week earlier, the rally had begun in Adelaide. In two days it had reached Western Australia. Now, five days further on, and the PlayStation convoy was still very much in Western Australia, with a lot of kilometres to be completed before they reached the Northern Territory.

The first two stages of Day Seven would be held along roads once used to stage the old Redex, Mobilgas and Ampol trials of a bygone era. Once upon a time, these were the main roads that helped link a nation, but as years rolled by most had been bypassed by newer, more modern constructions and left to fade away in the paddocks of the giant stations that dominate this slice of the world.

Sure, every now and again a station vehicle might have used them to access some remote part of the property, but what were once considered main thoroughfares are now nothing more than vague, teeth-rattling wheel tracks.

As if that wasn't enough, by the time the field arrived at the start of the first competitive stage, which ran along the old North-West Mail Road, there was the sun to contend with . . .

I heard a nice quote on the morning of Day Seven, from Ross Nicastri, who rejoined the PlayStation after having replacement parts for his Jackaroo engine sent up from Perth. The repairs had cost him a day-and-a-half's racing and made outright victory impossible, but he was still enthusiastic about completing the adventure.

'We had two options,' he said, 'either we keep going or we go back home to work. I know where I'd rather be.'

Ross had been described in a number of press releases as a former 'speedway ace'. I must confess that I'd never met him before the PlayStation, though from Day One I was extremely impressed with the way he handled his Jackaroo.

He is an off-road driver, not to be confused with rally drivers such as the world champion from the UK, Colin McRae, who we often see on TV roaring through forests on much smoother roads than we were confronting in outback Western Australia. In Australia, such rally roads usually run through forests and are normally located near the coast. Off-road racers, on the other hand, revel in the much rougher terrain: the sand dunes; the creek crossings; the corrugated, rocky stuff; the peaks and precipices.

Off-road drivers can drive very competently on rally-style roads. But this is not their passion. What they know best is how to drive very rapidly on really bad tracks.

Bruce Garland is your archetypal off-roader. And here he was laughing. 'Do you know, Brockie,' he reminded me again, always with a grin. 'We haven't even had a puncture yet!'

Unless you drive along Australia's west coast and see the incredibly isolated stretches of coastline and scrub first-hand, it's hard to fully appreciate the sheer scale and daunting distances that must have confronted those who first tried to explore this most lonely of lonely places. With most Australians remaining happily locked in their urban environment, it's only when you start the long and arduous climb up and along the Western Australian coast that the true enormity of the land we live in becomes breathtakingly obvious.

Amazing as it is, there are huge tracts of Australia—and most of them lie in Western Australia—that were not surveyed

At the start in Adelaide... just 22 days and more than 18,000 kilometres round Australia to the finish line.

We're away. A glistening 05 Jackaroo leads the PlayStation field away.

Clerk of the Course Bob Carpenter in Adelaide. Having surveyed the rally course three times, Bob, more than anyone, knew what was in store for the PlayStation field. Hence the grin...

The super-quick Subaru Impreza of Michael Guest and Jason Walk, which raced away from the field at the jump but crashed out of contention on day 3.

Station gates needed to be opened and closed, a task that often proved frustratingly difficult for my city-raised co-driver.

The 05 Jackaroo charges into Western Australia. Our run across the Nullarbor revealed that not only was the car surprisingly fast, it was also tough enough to withstand whatever the terrain threw at it.

Keith Callinan and Paul Couper in the VR Commodore that I had
driven in the 1995 round Australia rally. This was one of two factory
Holdens from that adventure which re-appeared in '98; the other, Ross
Dunkerton's old car, now belonged to my good mate, Peter Champion.

The ultra-tough and supremely well-driven Datsun 180B SSS of
David Lowe and Rob Gambino.

A quick stop, for a cuppa and a photo opportunity, and then we're back off the road.

The Bruce Garland/Harry Suzuki Jackaroo spraying up dust as we, and the rest of the PlayStation field, chase them all the way around Australia.

Back in 1966, Mini Cooper Ss were dominating at Bathurst. Twenty-two years later, Doug Coote, Cono Onofaro and their tough-as-they-come car attacked the rigours of the PlayStation Rally.

Bruce Garland, a renowned practical joker, gets beaten at his own game... falling victim to Chief Safety Officer Geoff Becker's elaborate, well-executed and highly-amusing 'drug test'.

Ross Nicastri, who led until his engine blew a piston on day 6 and later collided with two cows in the Northern Territory, showing off the scars of a brutally tough event.

Harry Suzuki, Bruce Garland's long-time co-driver.

Garland at the wheel of his Jackaroo, always smiling, always relishing this unique off-road experience.

A sheared steering bolt caused the Mini Cooper S to crash into two trees near Cairns. But still the adventure was not over; after a spell in the workshop (and a sleep-in for the weary drivers), the car rejoined the event as it raced down the Queensland coast.

You would not believe the different things I've been asked to autograph over the years! At Bathurst, during the PlayStation, we ran into one bloke who'd had me sign his chest a few years back, and then had the signature preserved forever as a tattoo. In contrast, being asked to autograph a Commodore glovebox is a much more standard request.

until early this century. One should never underestimate the guts and determination of those who first passed through these dangerous and desolate areas for the first time. For, as hard as we may have been finding the going in our modern four-wheel drives, how diabolical and dangerous must it have been for the pioneers who had only a couple of pack horses and a compass to keep them company in the days when there were no tracks?

Our starting time was just after 6.00 am, but the morning sun was blazing through the windscreen with a ferocity that belied the early hour. It was brutal, coming into the cockpit at such an angle that there was no avoiding its effects. For those lining up a little later, when the angle was less acute, it may not have been such a problem, but for the front runners it was akin to having ones eyes burnt out with a red-hot poker.

There was nothing to do but use one hand to shield my eyes and the other to steer. And yet it remained impossible to see. I was driving along a road I could only just see at the end of the bonnet while Webby did his best to warn me of what to expect in the distance.

The clouds of dust left by the Garland's Jackaroo, which had started just a minute in front of us, only compounded the problem. There were stages when, completely blind from the combination of the sun and the dust, we were obliged to almost come to a halt or risk hitting an obstacle we simply wouldn't have been able to see.

This was also a stage that held plenty of dangers for the unwary, or those prepared to take a chance, so we were happy to get out of it both intact and in good time.

This first stage, though, was just a taste of things to come. The second special stage, a 140 km trial, would be, we were told, an uncompromising test of both driving and navigational skills, along a narrow and at times vague track. Race organisers promised it was more suited to the stayers in the field rather than the sprinters, warning us that it would be one of the toughest of the entire rally.

The stage started from Winning Station, a property that covers a massive 750,000 hectares. The owners had set up a coffee, tea and cake stall near the starting line to help raise funds for local charity. And, as well as enjoying this morning tea, I took the opportunity to catch up with the station owners, who explained some of the trials and tribulations of running such a vast property.

These are the kind of Australians who always try to see the good in things. If they weren't naturally optimistic, they'd be wasting their time in the outback, because the outback is constantly testing them. In my view, without a shadow of doubt, their case is not being presented clearly to their fellow Australians back in the big cities. People in the bush are, by any stretch of the imagination, living and working out there because of the quality of life they seek, *not* because of the dollars they make. In truth, they are struggling. They are struggling financially, they are struggling even to reward themselves with the small luxuries city folk take for granted.

These people are innovative, intuitive, blessed with the ability to take life as it comes. If it rains, it rains. If it doesn't, we'll make do. With such a philosophy comes a glorious sense of freedom. Like the off-road driver, they deal only with the road in front of them, adapting to the conditions as they go.

Bruce Garland was first to depart the station, we were second. It was rough, but fast, and we were going like the clappers when, without warning, the sound of Bob Carpenter's voice came over the radio, trying to contact Bruce up ahead of us. Bob tried over and over again but to no avail. Webby contacted Bob on the radio and offered to try to reach the lead car on our two-way in the belief that because we were closer we might be able to get through and let Bruce know that Bob needed to talk to him.

What we didn't know at the time was that Bob was also in front of us, so he had as much chance as we did of contacting Bruce. As we'd already discovered, when Bruce was at speed in his Jackaroo there was no way he could hear his radio. Bob told us he was trying to inform Bruce that roughly 90 km of the stage had been scrapped at late notice. The course car that goes through the stage in front of the first race vehicle to check conditions up ahead, had come to the conclusion that one of the creek crossings on the second part of the stage had deteriorated to the point that none of the two-wheel drive vehicles would be able to get through. It was suggested that even a few of the 4 × 4s would have problems.

But Bruce ploughed on, unaware he was racing on through the wilderness for nothing aside from personal satisfaction, while the rest of the event stopped at the main road crossing at the 54 km mark of the stage.

The abandonment of the remainder of that stage left us with nothing but a long and dusty transport ride up the main road to the next service stop. Along the way, we wondered and pondered what had become or would become of Bruce. We also did our best to collide head on with the willy willys that danced their way across the highway. If one emerged out of the bush, you'd race to catch it up, to get close to it, feel it, touch it.

Eventually Bruce did turn up, more than a little bemused about how we'd all beat him home, but still extolling the brilliance of the stage.

He certainly wasn't angry. Instead, typically, he was laughing his head off. 'Brockie, you missed the best bit of road,' he hollered. 'Mate, the sand dunes across this creek, I was out of control!'

One competitive section remained for the day—and it was a beauty.

The transport stage, around 180 km long, took us to the outskirts of the massive Robe River Mine, a truly gigantic undertaking in the Hamersley Ranges. From there we set off on a rigorous test that started off rough, but evolved into a 100 km dash featuring some wide and death-defyingly fast roads. There were also plenty of crests to give up a few more frequent flyer points, and then over the last 10 km or so, we found ourselves on a tricky station track with some tough creek crossings to negotiate.

All in all, a stage with something for everyone.

Before the rally began, the Pilbara Tourist Association had reckoned the visit of the PlayStation to Port Hedland would generate more than $200,000 for the region. The local community saw the event as a means of boosting the income of local businesses and focusing attention on the region; they set out to provide a 'Big Day Out' atmosphere to welcome the cars into the town, and to give us all a Saturday night to remember.

It is difficult to convey to people from the big cities of the Australian east coast just what it meant to people in the out-back to have the chance to see the cars and meet the drivers. I was introduced to people who had driven two, three, four hundred, even a 1000 km to see cars surge through a creek or slide around a bend. You have to respect the fact that these people don't usually get a chance to see in person the cars and drivers they sometimes see on TV.

When the PlayStation field arrived in towns such as Port Hedland there was a terrific interaction between the drivers, crews and fans. Events such as this give us a chance to bring our sport to the people of Australia.

Motorsport is unique like that.

DAY 8

PORT HEDLAND
TO
CURTIN RAAF BASE

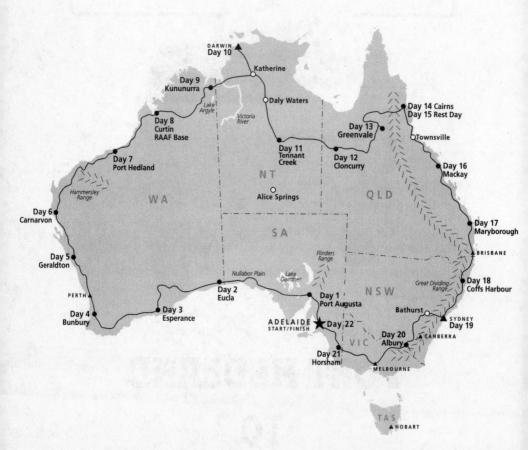

DARWIN
Day 10 ▲

○ Katherine

Day 9
Kununurra ●

Lake Argyle

● Daly Waters

Day 8
Curtin
RAAF Base ●

Victoria River

Day 7
Port Hedland ●

Day 11
Tennant
Creek ●

Day 13
Greenvale ●

Day 14 Cairns
Day 15 Rest Day ●

○ Townsville

Hammersley Range

Day 6
Carnarvon ●

N T

○ Alice Springs

Day 12
Cloncurry ●

Q L D

Day 16
Mackay ●

W A

S A

Day 17
Maryborough ●

Day 5
Geraldton ●

Flinders Range

▲ BRISBANE

Nullabor Plain

Lake Gairdner

PERTH ▲

Day 2
Eucla ●

Day 1
Port Augusta ●

N S W

Great Dividing Range

Day 18
Coffs Harbour ●

Day 4
Bunbury ●

Day 3
Esperance ●

Bathurst ○

▲ SYDNEY
Day 19

ADELAIDE
START/FINISH ★ **Day 22**

Day 20
Albury ●

▲ CANBERRA

V I C

Day 21
Horsham ●

▲ MELBOURNE

T A S

▲ HOBART

This was a day that would provide the entire PlayStation field with something of a relentless and particularly forbidding lesson in the history of Australian endurance rallying.

Two of the day's three stages would run along rough tracks that were once part of the main coastal road. It had been 45 years since these 'roads', were used for a round-Australia event. Indeed, the last time competition vehicles had rallied along here was in the 1954 Redex Trial. It wasn't until the 1998 PlayStation that the property owners who now have control of the land on which the old main highway runs again granted permission for outsiders to use the tracks for rallying.

The first stage was a 48 km run along a sandy two-wheel track, often only barely visible, running roughly 500 m inland and parallel to Eighty Mile Beach ...

During the rally, Bob Carpenter told me a lovely story about one of his trips to Western Australia, scouting territory in the months before the 1998 round-Australia rally. He came across one station owner just north of Port Hedland, who was astonished when Bob suggested he'd like the rally to go through his property.

'The bloke told us,' Bob recalled, 'how, as a five-year-old boy, he had stood with his Dad and watched Gelignite Jack Murray and other household names blast by the station bore on the same track we would be using in the '98 event.'

Webby and I had the honour of being the first car to experience this gentleman's homestead. I saw being first away as a big advantage, for it would mean that if nothing else, we wouldn't have to deal with any dust from the vehicles in front. And believe me, this really is an advantage.

Already in this event there had been several stages over which we'd made up huge chunks of time on the vehicles in front, only to find ourselves hitting the dust they had thrown into the air. It's not bad when a breeze is blowing, for it clears quite quickly, but in still conditions it can hang like an opaque curtain and make reading the road almost impossible. There is simply nothing else to do but back off and wait until you can see where you're going, for to press on blindly would be to invite an altercation with a piece of scenery that could spell the end of our adventure.

Having already lost a lot of time through that flat tyre on Day Three and our misadventure in the sand trap on Day Five, I knew that we could ill afford any more problems if we wanted to maintain a chance of winning this event. Even so, it was becoming clear that on our good days we simply weren't pegging back the advantage held by Bruce Garland at a rate that would give us a real shot at victory ... unless he hit a problem.

The initial part of the stage was fast and easy to read—often no more than a couple of sandy wheel tracks, but they were as plain as day. It was also very rough, but nothing that the Jackaroo couldn't handle. I thought we were going very well indeed.

However, about 27 km into the stage, we had to turn right and then quickly left off the main track onto an old section of road that would have tested the eyes of an eagle to follow. Several times I was driving along what we thought was the right path, only to have Webby yell over the intercom that we were either well to the right or well to the left of where we should have been.

This was really tough stuff, almost a case of blind man's buff at 150 km/h.

It all went wrong at the 34 km mark. In among the spinifex, there was supposed to be a right turn, marked by a hard-to-see, black-and-white painted post. However, when we arrived where it should've been, we found only a vague track but no post. I wanted to give the track a go, but Webby demanded we return to the main track. In his view, the right move was to go just a little further down the track to ensure we didn't turn too early.

From the very start of the event our trip computer, which gave Wayne measurements of total distance travelled, average speed and the distances between navigation instructions, had never proven to be completely accurate. Faced with our current dilemma, he wanted to be safe rather than sorry. I had to agree. To have started spearing down the wrong road, only to find, five, 10 or even 20 km later, that we had taken the wrong choice would have cost us much more time than simply heading a few hundred metres up another road to have good look around.

We went up the track for 300 m but there was still no black-and-white post. Then Bruce Garland's Jackaroo arrived on the scene, then a few other competitors as well, and we all engaged in a rather bizarre game of motorised hide'n'seek. If time had not been an issue, it would have been hilarious; from the air it would have appeared like something from a silent comedy movie, as vehicles ran around in circles looking for a post that, increasingly obviously, just wasn't there.

Finally, Bruce decided to start down the track that I had initially wanted to try. We all followed, thinking that, if he was on the right track then we were all okay, and that if he was wrong, then we were all lost. As things turned out, it was the right way. We ended up dropping a little time, but nothing drastic.

The second stage of the day was a 102 km leg that started not far away from the Sandfire Roadhouse, which was also a service point during the 1979 Repco Trial. I remember that back then the stop at the roadhouse presented one of the rare opportunities on the event to grab a shower, which I did in one of the motel rooms. However, 19 years later we stopped for just 15 minutes, so even a shower was out of the question.

Let me tell you, a shower would have been very welcome. As we headed north the temperature continued to rise; blessed as we were with a vehicle where the air conditioning had been removed in a bid to save precious kilograms, the inside of the Jackaroo had all the creature comforts of an oven. I hate to think what the temperature was inside the vehicle, but after each and every stage both Webby and I looked as if we'd stopped somewhere along the way to have a shower ... with our clothes on.

In conditions such as this it's vital to keep up the intake of fluids or risk the very real possibility of dehydration, so we were gulping down water chilled in a small esky mounted just behind the front seats. Water is the key to life in outback areas such as this, for while a human can survive for a surprising length of time without food, lack of water means a rapid end. Thankfully, the team was supplying us with so much liquid that we were more in danger of drowning rather than dehydrating.

The first 50 km of the second stage of the day were run over what was once, millions of years ago, the seabed. It was flat, salty, fast and, in places, rough. We'd been told that when wet, the tracks around here can get outrageously slippery, but given the baking sun, that wasn't going to be a factor in this rally at least.

Nature has an incredible way of throwing in the occasional and truly inexplicable wild card and at one stage we splashed through one of its most baffling offerings. Despite the fact that what once was sea is now land, the ocean, or at least its influence, remains. The track crossed a clear saltwater creek— running with nothing but pure salty and completely undrink- able sea water and lined with ocean mangroves. Sure, there are saltwater creeks everywhere on the coast and mangroves are nothing special . . . well, most times anyway. But when the ocean is 46 km away? Certainly this is the only place in Australia, and some experts believe in the world, where this happens.

Later in the stage, we had to drive onto and then around a huge claypan. We had to be somewhat circumspect, and follow the two wheel marks. Even then, it was so slippery that each change in direction resulted in huge, all but out-of- control slides as the Jackaroo battled for traction. It was clear that if we slipped off the established path, there was a huge chance we'd be bogged, axle-deep in trouble. Heaven knows what it was like for the competitors in two-wheel drive cars.

Still, this was great fun, as I threw the Jackaroo into long sideways drifts along the track. But just feeling how boggy even the hard areas of the claypan were curtailed any temptation to try a shortcut on a corner.

Eventually, as we got closer to the coast, the terrain dried out. Up ahead, we saw the dust plumes of Bruce's car, meandering along what was clearly a twisty track up ahead, and thought, 'You beauty, we're catching him'. Then I had an idea. The ground looked pretty harmless, so while Bruce stuck to the winding road, I pointed our Jackaroo at his dust and headed straight for him. Within minutes, I was right on his tail.

The track eventually returned to the old coastal road which, over the course of decades, has managed to dig itself down into the sand. The end result is a road that runs between two walls of sand, meaning there is no chance of overtaking unless you can transform your vehicle into a helicopter.

And that's why we struck trouble. With Bruce leading and me right up his backside chasing, we turned onto the old highway only to discover an old flatbed truck lumbering along at near walking pace. The dust was so thick that we could barely see Bruce, and he was quick to jump on the radio to warn us to slow down dramatically. Webby, realising that those chasing us would soon be in the same situation, relayed the call back through the field.

I really am talking about a single lane lined with near-vertical walls of sand, there was just no way around. That meant the stage was dead and buried, for in the choking dust the field started to concertina and found itself motoring along at very low speeds, following the mystery truck.

With the increasing traffic jam, Webby tried to contact Clerk of the Course Bob Carpenter on the satellite phone to seek advice, but was unable to get through. So the leading competitors took a vote—hey, this is democracy at work—to abandon the stage, though that decision was later overruled by Bob Carpenter and his team.

Not long after we had accepted the inevitable, the truck pulled over! Out hopped a few blokes who had been camping on the banks of a river on a fishing expedition and who had heard that the rally would be coming past. They'd decided to motor on out to have a look at the rally as it passed by. Trouble was, by the time they hit the road, they managed only to destroy the stage completely. They'd been crawling up the road to their preferred vantage point, blissfully unaware that the entire field of the PlayStation Rally was banking up behind them.

Thus we came to a rather unsatisfactory end to the rally for the day. But at least the early finish gave me a chance to get on the satellite phone to catch up with what was happening in the Sandown 500 touring-car race in Melbourne. I wanted to find out how the Holden lads, Mark Skaife and Craig Lowndes, were getting on without me. Probably better than ever if the case be known.

I called Skaifey on his mobile and found him standing in the pits, while Craig was out in the car and leading the race. Funnily enough, while we were sweating it out in temperatures well above 40 degrees Celsius, it was cold and *very* wet in Melbourne. I reckon I was in the right place, and just to make sure everyone at Sandown heard about how good the weather was at the top of Western Australia, I did a live cross to the circuit announcers, who broadcast our chat over the PA system. I also managed a quick chat to John Bowe. Just how the hardy souls—soggy and shivering in the stand at Sandown— took the news that we were belting along under a perfectly clear blue sky and moaning about the heat remains a mystery, but I imagine that most of them would have happily traded places.

But I wouldn't have. The PlayStation was proving to be a brilliant event, and the fact that we stopped each night made it possible to catch up with spectators and fans around the nation. And also with our fellow competitors, which was a nice change from the 1979 Repco event. Then it seemed that we never stopped at all and the only thing that most spectators saw was a cloud of dust, a car flashing past at top speed, and then another cloud of dust. In contrast, the PlayStation allowed an interaction between the crews and the public, and I was really enjoying the chance to catch up with people everywhere we went.

Having said all this, at our stop on Day Eight there would be no public. Instead, we would be guests of the Australian military, staying at Curtin RAAF base, 30 km south-east of Derby. The base is run by a handful of RAAF staff, whose job entails keeping the place up to scratch so that, at a moment's notice, it can handle full-scale military operations. In fact, this base can be at full combat readiness in less than 24 hours, should circumstances demand it.

Given that no one has tried to invade recently, for most of the time the base sits silent, practically deserted. When we first drove through the gates, the feeling was akin to entering a ghost town. Most recently, Curtin has been used as a holding facility for boat people discovered landing on Australian shores or bobbing around in our territorial waters.

The base itself is huge and, as we were to discover, incredibly well-equipped. At first we believed that, for the first time on the trip, we would have to break out our swags, but that wasn't to be. Because Curtin can immediately be transformed from ghost base to the home of an RAAF strike force, there is more than ample accommodation. This consists of long rows of demountable buildings with small rooms that can sleep two people, on bunks, in air-conditioned comfort. I claimed one for myself, Webby grabbed the one next door and then we headed for the shower block to wash away the dust and dirt of another day on the road.

Well, at least *I* headed to the shower block. Webby, Bruce Garland, Harry Suzuki and a few of the others had discovered a makeshift bar that had been set up by the Derby police to raise money for local charity. Obviously they saw it as their duty to try to contribute as much as possible to the local community, and if that entailed sinking a few cold VBs then they were only too willing to make the sacrifice. Such unselfish behaviour!

Dinner that night was served in the mess hall, which really can look after a battalion, but our fare was prepared on an open fire outside. Just how the locals managed to whip up such a huge selection of roast meats, vegetables and desserts over an open fire is truly amazing.

Every so often we heard an explosion but, never fear, it was merely Bruce Garland letting some more firecrackers off. Here was a great chance for all the competitors and crews to mingle. But with no outside distractions to keep them amused, it also promoted some evil doings as the night dragged on.

Ross Nicastri, aided by Webster I am reliably informed, found the room occupied by Garland and hatched an evil plan. I don't know how many people out there are familiar with racetape but, take it from me, this stuff is incredibly strong. Over the years it's held more race cars together than welding. It can hold down the bonnet of a touring car travelling at almost 300 km/h down Conrod Straight at Bathurst. So Ross reckoned it would easily hold a door closed.

And so they taped the door to Bruce's room closed. With the windows shut to keep the air-conditioned air inside, and adorned with fly-screen mesh too, the race leader was now a prisoner in his own room. I heard the giggling from my room but chose not to investigate, which is probably just as well for I could have copped the same treatment. Despite the noise, Bruce was still punching out the Z's and blissfully unaware of his predicament.

Indeed, he would sleep peacefully for a couple more hours

until, awoken by an urgent call of nature, he tried to leave his room to head for the outdoor toilets. He pushed at the door. He pulled at the door. He hit the door with his shoulder and turned the handle with increasing desperation, but still nothing happened. At this stage, a combination of the sweat of exertion and bursting bladder desperation was pushing him to superhuman feats of strength, but still the door remained firmly closed. Bruce decided to summon help by both screaming—and I can attest that it was like the cry of a trapped wild animal—and hitting the wall of his bedroom-cum-prison with a ferocity that shook the entire building and would have woken the dead.

But help, it seemed, couldn't come fast enough. So, in an inspired piece of Aussie ingenuity, Bruce took the only option that was remaining, forced open a window, gave the fly-screen mesh a nudge and allowed nature to take its course through the narrow gap he'd created.

Thus, by the time those summoned by his maniacal screams did manage to remove the swathe of racetape and free him, they found him lying on the bed with a strangely peaceful look upon his face.

This act of war, of course, prompted Bruce to promise retribution upon all those responsible. 'I'm going to blow Nicastri up with a bunger when he least expects it,' he told anyone who would listen. Meanwhile, I went to great pains before the early start next morning to disassociate myself from the prank.

I didn't want Bruce watching me too closely, for I had something up my sleeve for him when we reached Darwin . . . now only two days away.

DAY 9

CURTIN RAAF BASE
TO
KUNUNURRA

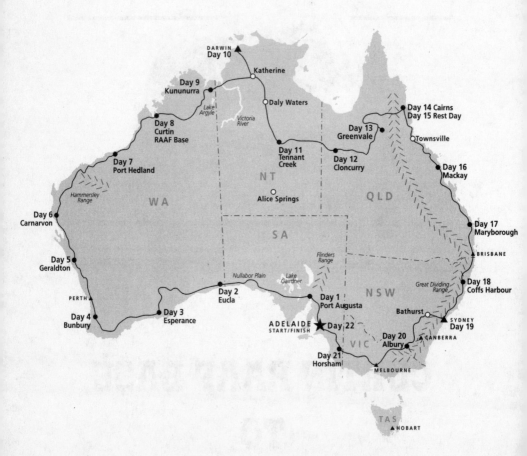

DARWIN
Day 10

Katherine

Day 9
Kununurra

Lake
Argyle

Day 8
Curtin
RAAF Base

Day 7
Port Hedland

Hammersley
Range

Victoria
River

Daly Waters

Day 14 Cairns
Day 15 Rest Day

Townsville

Day 13
Greenvale

Day 11
Tennant
Creek

Day 12
Cloncurry

Day 16
Mackay

WA

NT

Alice Springs

QLD

Day 17
Maryborough

Day 6
Carnarvon

SA

BRISBANE

Day 5
Geraldton

Nullabor Plain

Lake
Gairdner

Flinders
Range

Day 18
Coffs Harbour

PERTH

Day 2
Eucla

Day 1
Port Augusta

Great Dividing
Range

NSW

Bathurst

Day 4
Bunbury

Day 3
Esperance

ADELAIDE
START/FINISH

Day 22

SYDNEY
Day 19

CANBERRA

Day 20
Albury

VIC

Day 21
Horsham

MELBOURNE

TAS

HOBART

Bruce Garland's lead stood at around 30 minutes, with the Brock Jackaroo in second spot. Sure, there was still a long way to go in the event—the field hadn't even reached the halfway point yet—but most observers believed that unless Garland made a major error or suffered a mechanical problem, the best the remainder of the field could hope for was second place.

Moving into third place was the Holden Commodore ute of Graeme Wise, who had slowly worked his way through the field by driving with his head rather than his right foot.

Ross Nicastri's charge had come to a grinding halt a couple of days before, when he lost a piston in his Jackaroo, had to be towed out of a stage and a big penalty which had dropped him out of the running. Some hastily procured spares had allowed him to continue, but the fact that he had been forced to miss a day's competition to chase and catch the field meant that he was now competing purely for fun.

As the field rolled up for the start of Day Nine, fourth place was now in the hands of Keith Callinan, driving the VR Commodore that Brock had used in the 1995 round-Australia rally. Indeed two of the factory Holdens from '95—Brock's car and the one driven by Ross Dunkerton—were still running in the '98 epic. Peter Champion was in Dunkerton's old car.

Peter Champion is a sensational guy. Bev and I have been to stay with him and his family several times. Peter owns his own mine, is a sub-contractor to a number of big coal mines in Queensland, and is one of those guys who just rolls up his sleeves and gets things done regardless of the obstacles in his way. A real self-made man is Peter.

Originally from Tasmania, Peter and his brother left as young kids to make their fortune. He started off with just a couple of battered tractors, an old truck and some contract work to repair roads for local plant owners and the shire council. He gradually built his business up from that.

He, his wife and his young children lived in a tiny caravan, 40 km from the general store. It wasn't a good idea to forget anything when you did the shopping. He is living proof that in this country of ours you can do what you dream of doing if you are prepared to get out there and have a go. Opportunities are available, you can actually make it happen. He's also a superb example of another great Aussie trait—he'd gladly give the shirt off his own back to help the less fortunate fellow next to him.

Nowadays, he's a very successful businessman, who has been able to accumulate a wonderful collection of cars, including a number of my Commodores. He has about 10 or 12 of them, either race cars or the special road cars built during the 1980s, and a replica of the Austin A30 in which I started my circuit-racing career.

Peter Champion applies many of the values that are an integral part of endurance rallying to his business. He's always fair dinkum with people, never does the dirty on them, and is a person of great principles. He's outrageously fastidious— I have visited his mine and seen up to a dozen trucks, precisely lined up and hosed down, looking glistening and gleaming despite the fact they've been working on the mine all day. He runs his rally cars like that, too. Everything has to be right.

At this stage, however, he wasn't even driving his car, having handed over to a relief driver while he flew back to his mine in Queensland, which had been closed down because of massive flooding. Not surprisingly, with a huge contract to supply coal to Japan to be met, Peter had decided his presence was needed back at the mine. When you have millions of dollars worth of machinery and a huge crew just standing around with nothing to do but watch flood waters rise, it doesn't take long for profit to quickly become loss.

Meanwhile, Keith Callinan was going great guns in my old car from the '95 round-Australia. The thought did cross my mind, more than once, that a Commodore could make it through three round-Australia rallies in a row. Certainly if Graeme Wise in his ute and Callinan stayed in touch with the leading Jackaroos, or if Bruce or I had major dramas, we could be in trouble.

I didn't know a great deal about Graeme Wise, who is a fairly quiet sort of guy away from his car. However, his driving and achievements in the rally spoke volumes of his ability. For quite a few years he has been one of the guys to beat in the Victorian rally scene and I have no doubts that given a chance, in the right equipment, he'd make an impact nationally against the likes of Toyota's ace Neal Bates and Subaru's flying kiwi, Possum Bourne. And there was no doubting that the Pedder's ute that Wise was sharing with Linda Long had the potential to mix it with the Jackaroos over the smoother stages.

We knew when we began that this was going to be yet another long, hard and hot day at the office, for there was 1005 km to put under our wheels before we reached Kununarra.

The first stage ran through the spectacular McClintock Ranges, on very slippery roads that featured lots of washaways and overhanging eucalypts whose shadows often camouflaged the perils of the road. In several places the road was covered with little round rocks—no more than about four or five mm in diameter, that made it feel as if you were driving on ice.

Eventually, we arrived at the massive Ruby Plains Station, one of the incredibly huge chunks of Australia owned by the legendary cattle company S. Kidman and Co. Founded by the famed cattle king, Sir Sidney Kidman, this company takes up vast tracts of Australia and has made an incredible success out of raising cattle in some of the most inhospitable parts of the country.

How did they ever do it? Let's just sit back in our capital cities today and wonder how people ever managed to survive through the deprivation and hardship these people must have encountered. How did their children get adequate food and shelter? What did they do for education? What they achieved is extraordinary and demonstrates that when a person gets an idea and enough supporters jump on board just about anything is possible. And think of the pace at which their enterprises developed. Everything about life today is now, now, now. The pioneers couldn't have thought like that.

In a battling spirit not too dissimilar to that which inspired those great Australians of the past, Mark Griffith, an independent tyre dealer from Brisbane, continued to hammer away in a little Toyota RAV4 that he had literally cobbled together in the days before the start. A good-humoured, easy-going and most likeable guy, Mark had put his contender for the round-Australia together in record time, and judging by the way he was going, he'd done a brilliant job. Sure, the little two-litre, four-cylinder-engined Toyota didn't have the speed to match some of the faster four-wheel drives, but he was obviously driving it to the limit and remained in the hunt.

Unfortunately, the final stage of the day had to be cancelled. It was going to be run in the Bow River cattle station, a property owned and run by Aborigines, and it was going to be tough. Really tough. Indeed, when Bob Carpenter first went through this area looking for stages for the event, he actually rejected the tracks on this property as being simply too tough—even for the four-wheel drives. But, eager to help with the rally, elders of the tribe had promised to have the tracks graded in time for the PlayStation to pass through. Bad weather, however, had intervened and the track improvements had not been possible.

One of Day Nine's service stops was at Halls Creek, famous in Australian history as the site where gold was first discovered in Western Australia back in the late 1800s. The locals were out in force during our quick stopover and, as usual, the hospitality of rural Australia was extraordinary.

Ask an old-time rally enthusiast about Halls Creek, and they think of the Redex Trials. And dust, shattered suspensions, blown tyres and tall tales. The heat, the flies, boiling radiators, lack of creature comforts. It's part of the 'wild' west.

Off the beaten track it's still hot and dusty, but the town itself looks pretty good today. I went for a quick wander down to the souvenir stalls, then to an art display, then to the Aboriginal welfare centre, to get a feel for the place. I had a yarn with one of the locals, the owner of a service station, 'How are you getting on? How are things going?'

The response was typical of these parts. 'Ah, no worries, you know, things are looking pretty good.' But then you chat a bit more and find out that, well, yeah, things are a bit tough. 'Not as many trucks and buses coming through now,' he told me.

But, generally speaking, they are people who won't be defeated.

Kununurra is situated at the centre of the massive Ord River irrigation scheme and offers some of the most breathtaking scenery you could ever hope to see. Now a thriving community, it was created in the mid-1960s to act as a base for workers employed in the creation of the Ord River scheme, which dammed the river to allow farming in what was once a barren wasteland.

The dam created Lake Argyle, and if you reckon Sydney Harbour holds a fair amount of water, think again. Lake Argyle is almost 10 times the size of Sydney Harbour and has become the home to an incredible and extensive array of birds and other wildlife. Certainly, the greenery that springs up around the lake makes Kununurra an oasis in a tough, mountainous landscape. After a day of belting through the desert, it came as welcome relief. I, for one, didn't mind the fact that we had to skip one of the stages and would be arriving a little early.

Later that evening, I had an opportunity to talk to members of the local Aboriginal community, who gave me an insight into their way of life beyond that provided by the media. One woman related experiences of her life as an Aboriginal in a white community. She told me how many of her friends and family had originally been based in areas closer to the coastline. That was their home. But they had shifted across to Kununurra because of the infrastructure that had been built up to service the major redevelopments of the 1960s and '70s.

'How is life here?' I asked her.

'Not too bad,' she responded, before going on to explain how some kids appeared to be struggling with the demands of living in a town the size of Kununurra.

'They lose their way, their Aboriginal heritage?' I suggested.

'Well, I guess they do,' she nodded, but then said, 'I really can't say any more to you. I have said too much already.'

'Why is that?' I asked.

'I am only allowed to talk to you about these matters in the presence of an Aboriginal elder,' she explained.

'I wasn't aware of that,' I said. 'My apologies, I don't understand the Aboriginal protocol.'

This woman wasn't being rude, evasive or cautious. She was simply explaining a fact of her life. I thought to myself, as she walked away, you can travel anywhere in this country thinking you know how things work ... and every day you find out something new. What a fascinating approach to life: it's not for you to bluntly get out there and express your opinions. Before you blindly state your case to the world, you need to have your views okayed by the members of the community who have learnt the ways of the world.

Respect for those who are older and wiser cannot be a bad thing. Western society has gone the opposite way. It proposes that youth is all there is. If you are old, you are off the pace, you don't understand life any more. Aborigines take a totally different view.

Although this woman spoke to me only briefly, her reticence and respect for her elders taught me plenty about the Aboriginal way of life. I reckon Aborigines have a stronger sense of their community than other cultures. And they recognise much better than many others that the strength, health and vitality of the community depends on all the individuals who make it up, the respect they have for each other and the great respect they have for those who have inherited positions of influence and authority.

Another thing I did, later in the night at a sponsor's function, was to walk over and sit down next to an Aboriginal couple who had come along but were sitting near the exit, well away from the main tables.

'How are you getting on?' I asked, grabbing a chair, to which one of them replied quietly, 'Look, are you sure you should be sitting down with us?'

'What do you mean?' I was confused. I wasn't grandstanding, just wanted a quick chat.

'Well,' the other one said, 'everyone is looking.'

'Why is that?' I asked.

'You are European and we are black. Are you sure you should be here?'

'Yeah, I'm sure,' I said flatly, 'I am just a person who is curious about life. Do you mind talking to me?'

'No, not at all,' one said with a slight grin. 'If you don't mind, we don't mind. But we thought you might be embarrassed, because people are looking at you and saying, why aren't you over talking with us.'

'I can talk to them any time,' I said. And we continued on with what for me was a rewarding and interesting conversation.

DAY 10

KUNUNURRA
TO
DARWIN

DARWIN
Day 10

Katherine

Day 9
Kununurra

Lake
Argyle

Day 8
Curtin
RAAF Base

Daly Waters

Victoria
River

Day 14 Cairns
Day 15 Rest Day

Townsville

Day 13
Greenvale

Day 7
Port Hedland

Day 11
Tennant
Creek

Day 12
Cloncurry

N T

Day 16
Mackay

Hammersley
Range

W A

Alice Springs

Q L D

Day 6
Carnarvon

S A

Day 17
Maryborough

Day 5
Geraldton

Flinders
Range

BRISBANE

PERTH

Nullabor Plain

Lake
Gairdner

Day 2
Eucla

Day 1
Port Augusta

N S W

Great Dividing
Range

Day 18
Coffs Harbour

Day 4
Bunbury

Day 3
Esperance

Bathurst

SYDNEY
Day 19

ADELAIDE
START/FINISH

Day 22

CANBERRA

Day 20
Albury

V I C

Day 21
Horsham

MELBOURNE

T A S

HOBART

After a week in Western Australia, it was finally time to move into the Northern Territory. The PlayStation crossed the border not long after leaving Kununurra, but aside from waving goodbye to speed restrictions, not much else changed.

Before proceedings began for the day, race leader Bruce Garland explained why things were going so smoothly for him. To this point, he revealed proudly, he only needed to replace a couple of brake pads.

'The trick is to minimise the risks,' Garland said. 'I've been driving at between 50 and 70 per cent and that's the thing to do. Every time I've attacked a course in the past it's all turned to crap, because that's when your risk factors multiply.

'So you keep at one pace that doesn't hurt the car—fast enough to keep an eye on what the others are doing, but let them get into trouble.'

Garland's preparations had been meticulous. He even admitted to rehearsing for the stage out of Perth on Day Five, which was conducted on the road used for the Western Australian leg of the World Rally Championship, by playing a computer game based on that rally course.

The soaring temperatures in the top end were really making life difficult. The fact that our car didn't have air conditioning was compounded by the fact that we had to race with the windows up on special stages or risk suffocating in the dust.

Oddly enough, during the competitive stages themselves I really didn't notice the temperature, because I was focused on driving, and that really did require 100 per cent concentration.

However, at the end of the stage the heat hit you like a hammer blow and Webby and I were drinking water at a prodigious rate. The trick is—and this applies to those on a holiday jaunt as much as it does for those in competition—to keep on drinking. Don't wait until you get thirsty, for by that stage it's too late.

The first stage of Day 10 was run over a couple of typical top-end cattle stations, Rosewood and Amanbidgee, which are both run by Aborigines. Of course, running through cattle stations meant that there would inevitably be cattle on the roads at some stage, especially as we passed close to the bores. There was also the prospect of gates to open and close; for stock diseases are a major factor up here, and one stray beast could cause financial disaster.

Frankly, I didn't have a problem with gates. Why should I? This was Webby's job, and not one that he particularly relished. It entailed him leaping from the vehicle, running, opening the gate, then closing it when I had driven through. Although station owners went to great lengths to leave as many gates as possible open, allowing the competitors to pass through without having to stop, there were some cases where this simply wasn't feasible.

One thing that Webby, very much a city boy, did have to learn was that in the outback no two gates are ever the same. Certainly none have the type of locking mechanism found on the front gate of your typical suburban house; locals up here are always inventing new and often complicated methods to ensure that once a gate is shut, it remains shut.

While regular competitors in outback events such as the Australian Safari have learned to deal with most gates, each one we encountered was a new adventure for my navigator. His enthusiasm to get them open and closed as fast as possible

One of the many willy-willys we saw as we headed north through Western Australia.

One of Australia's most famous watering holes ... the Daly Waters Pub.

With Bruce Garland at the bar of the Daly Waters Pub.

A common sight in the Territory... and one to be avoided by tourists, locals and PlayStation Rally drivers alike.

The husband-and-wife team of Neville and Shirley Hawkins and their Toyota LandCruiser, a long and dusty way from the North Queensland home base of their sponsor, Tully Bananas.

Back in 1980-81, HDT Special Vehicles constructed just 500 modified Commodore SL/Es. You can imagine my surprise when I saw this one - in magnificent condition, nearly two decades later, in Cloncurry, Qld! - during the PlayStation. Note the number plate.

Another keen Brock fan, this time in Mt Isa. Again, note the number plate, which reflects not just the fact that this is a North Queensland Fire Safety Service truck.

The children of Hughenden, in central Queensland, were given the day off school to see the PlayStation field hit town, which created a real carnival atmosphere ... and a long queue for autographs!

The service given by Bruce Garland's support crew was first-class and unwavering, a key factor in our 1-2 finish.

Similarly impressive was the event's organisation. Here the lead car of Garland/Suzuki passes through one of the rally's many checkpoints.

The Commodore of Peter Champion and Ken Long in full flight.

The Pedders Commodore Ute of Graeme Wise and Linda Long, which was cruising in third place until a series of major setbacks in North Queensland.

The back number plate of our Jackaroo. Bruce Garland's enterprising crew made a few dollars selling replicas during the event.

Adventurers all. A competitors group shot, taken on day 20, near Lithgow.

No-one begrudged Bruce's great triumph, least of all Webby (top left) and me. We knew how hard he, Harry Suzuki (top right) and his crew (in front) had worked to achieve this brilliant result.

was clearly obvious, but his expertise in the matter left much to be desired.

This was an incredibly tough stage, for although the roads were wide, they were also incredibly rough and covered in sharp rocks that were absolute murder on the tyres. This made me thankful that we were running on purpose-made Bridgestone competition tyres, which had kevlar belting on the sidewalls to—hopefully—stop the rocks cutting through. There was also a second line of defence. The tyres were full of mousse, a bright pink liquid that, if the tyre did indeed suffer a puncture, was designed to seal the hole and hold the pressure up until the end of the stage. It had already saved us on several occasions.

But not everyone had the same luck as we did . . .

Graeme Wise suffered three flat tyres—two during the first stage and one on the transport section that followed, while Keith Callinan's Commodore blew no less than four tyres on this stage. With only two spares at his disposal, poor Keith had to beg for tyres at the roadside, flagging down drivers and relying on their generosity.

Fortunately, he managed to find enough rubber to continue—by now he was getting really good at changing tyres. But then, when one of the vehicles he had borrowed a tyre from itself had a flat further on down the stage, they flagged down Keith to get their spare back! By the end of that 81 km stage, Keith's legendary good humour and happy disposition were stretched to their very limit.

It wasn't unusual to come roaring over a crest or sliding around a corner to find the track covered in wall-to-wall cattle. They aren't particularly bright, so more often that not, instead of running to the side of the road at the sight of a four-wheel drive Jackaroo blazing towards them, horn blowing, the cattle would instead trot down the middle of the track. This meant using the Jackaroo to round them up and herd them away so we could find a way through.

Unfortunately, Ross Nicastri didn't get it quite right and ended up hitting two cows on this stage. Although the cows were big, Ross' Jackaroo is bigger, and the beasts came off second best. But this only earnt Ross a $600-plus bill from the owner of the poor beasts.

Another casualty was the Toyota RAV4 driven by Mark Griffith and Del Garbett, who had been running in fifth place until they lost 90 minutes after suffering rear suspension and front strut problems.

After this stage, we faced a 430 km transport leg to Katherine, passing Timber Creek along the way. The last time I was at Timber Creek was during one of the Variety Club Bashes, where we stayed at the local Aboriginal Health Care Centre. I remember a few of the locals offered to take John Farnham and me out fishing. John is a mad-keen fisherman, and despite the fact that we had to get up in what seemed like the middle of the night, it proved to be an offer well worth taking up. We headed out into the Victoria River in search of barramundi and I remember thinking that, judging by the number of crocs in the area, we weren't the only ones out looking for a feed.

We both hooked a barrumundi before having to get back to start the Bash again. I'd been a little smart and organised a Channel 7 helicopter to pick us up and get us to the start of the day's stage in time. In fact, I had to get to the start of that stage, at a crossing downstream, because someone had pledged $3000 to the Variety Club to be my co-driver for the stage from the river crossing back to Timber Creek. So it was a simple case of reel my line in, pack the fishing gear up, stroll over a couple of hills by 7.00 am, to where I'd arranged for the chopper to pick us up, and jump in next to the pilot.

I remember being in that chopper on the way to the start of that special stage, thundering down the Victoria River just a couple of metres above the water, and thinking that I was in a scene from the film *Apocalypse Now*. No doubt, that's what the fishermen a little further downstream thought too when he raced past them, just over their heads. We came up on them so quickly, out of absolutely nowhere on a beautifully quiet morning, they must have believed they were under attack.

By 9.00 am I was back at Timber Creek to share stories of the fishing, helicopter and driving adventures. You can really pack a few things in to a morning in this country!

Back to the PlayStation . . .

At Timber Creek, we stopped at the Mobil roadhouse—a pub, restaurant, motel and service station all in one. Hanging over the petrol bowsers is the skin of a monster croc, a reminder of why you don't go swimming in the Victoria River no matter how hot it gets. Around here, the locals call anyone stupid enough to tempt fate and take a dip in the river just one thing . . . bait. It's much better, they argue, to remain hot and dry than end up as breakfast.

They've got a great sense of humour out here. For me, the sign over the door of the public bar just about summed up the dry wit that is so typically Australia. It read: 'Free Beer Tomorrow'. Put there especially for all the rally drivers passing through.

Thanks fellas!

Eventually we reached the service stop at Katherine show-ground. Back in 1997, the town of Katherine was totally flooded. It was a disaster, and when we stopped near the service point at the showground on the edge of town, from the marks high up on the trees we could see just how high the water had actually risen.

Because there are no speed limits in the Northern Territory, outside the towns, we made cracking time into Katherine. But we then faced a long and hot wait by the roadside until we could check-in for servicing—there were penalties for those who arrive early just as there were for those who arrive late. Webby and I had parked under the shade of a tree, resigned to sweltering, when the master salesman himself, Ed Mulligan, arrived in one of our Jackaroo service vehicles and told us to follow him back up the road. Ed had done a deal with the owners of the local caravan park to let us use their pool for some much-needed cooling down. The price? A few P. Brock autographs on some posters.

Believe me, this was a small price to pay to escape the heat. When we arrived, Bruce Garland and Harry Suzuki were already splashing around, and Graeme Wise and his co-driver, Linda Long, were not far behind us. Just half an hour in the water was all it took to rejuvenate our weary bodies, which was just as well for there were three more stages left to run during the afternoon before we headed into Darwin ... three stages that I was really looking forward to.

After days of dirt, we were about to tackle the only three all bitumen special stages of the entire 18,000 km event. The three stages were all to be held on sections of the old Stuart Highway. Two were on parts no longer used, while the piece of road used for the third section is now a tourist drive. I could see why, for the scenery was spectacular, although I was in a little bit too much of a hurry to give it my full attention.

I was eager to have a blast down the bitumen, although I wasn't really expecting the Jackaroo to be in the hunt. After all, it was big, heavy and had a high centre of gravity. So, while these three stages would be good for a laugh we knew some of the cars should give us a real hammering.

And that was indeed the case, although we did hold our own. Indeed, on the longest of the three stages—almost 31 km—we all but caught Bruce, who started a minute in front of us. Even though we weren't fastest, boy, did we have fun. On one stage the road dropped down to a sweeping right-hander before it headed back up the hill. Bob Carpenter was watching from inside the corner and reckoned I had my inside front wheel about 20 cm off the ground from the moment we turned into the corner to when we were at the top of the hill.

Then it was off towards Darwin, where we'd organised to have a surprise waiting for Bruce.

My brother Phil has lived in Darwin for several years. He was, of course, a very handy touring-car racer and was a team-mate of mine at Bathurst before he headed off to do other things.

I was keen to play a practical joke on Bruce and enlisted Phil's help. With the help of Webby and a cooperative Channel 7 film crew, we came up with a plan we reckoned would stop Bruce in his tracks.

We arrived at Darwin's Stokes Hill Wharf, where a couple of navy frigates were moored, and our evil scheme went into action. The Channel 7 crew began interviewing Bruce immediately after he stepped from his vehicle. Suddenly, a young lady carrying a small child burst from the crowd.

'Bruce, Bruce, I knew you would come back,' she gushed. 'Meet your son, I've told him all about you.'

All the colour drained from Bruce's face, while the TV cameras kept rolling and a myriad of cameras clicked away. The poor bloke battled for something—anything—to say.

'Don't you remember me, the last time you were in Darwin you said you would come back,' she continued, until, unable to hold back, she broke into laughter.

I reckon it was a great 'gotcha', a real classic, and I had to give Phil full accolades for putting it all together in record time.

In the 1979 Repco, it was in Darwin that we enjoyed the first and only rest day of the entire event. I can remember walking through the front door of the Travelodge Hotel, where we were staying, going straight through the foyer to the pool area and jumping straight in ... clothes and all. I was covered in so much dust that the water around me turned a murky brown, while people sunbaking around the pool watched in horror as the rest of the team did the same thing. By the time we were all in, the pool looked more like a mud puddle.

This time we were staying at the 'Centra' Hotel, but when we pulled up outside, the memories came flooding back. The Centra was indeed the very same hotel, except for its new name. This time, though, I didn't walk out and fall into the pool, but I did hand over a jumbo-sized bag of washing that the hotel promised me would be cleaned and dried in near-record time.

Funny how things change over two decades. In 1979, all I cared about was getting cool. Now, I was more concerned that I would have enough clean clothes.

I hope this means I'm getting neat and not old.

DAY 11

DARWIN
TO
TENNANT CREEK

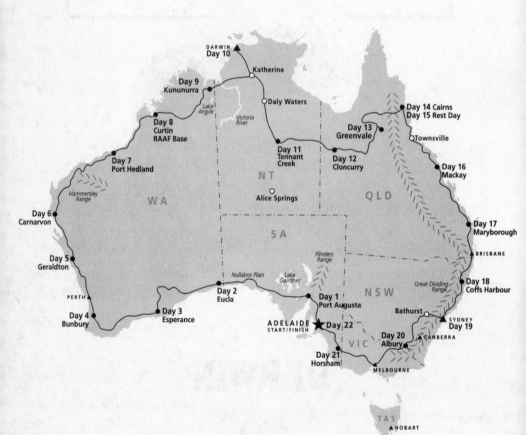

'Off-road, long-distance racing is like cricket,' Bruce Garland explained to a reporter before the commencement of Day 11. 'Sometimes you bring out your fast bowlers, sometimes your slow ones. Sometimes you use the sun.

'Today, I'll use the dust!'

Garland knew where the PlayStation was heading: through steep hills, over slippery, rocky and disconcertingly dusty ground, made ultra-tricky for part of the stage's 37 km by the jungle of trees that often engulfed the track.

For the cars behind Garland's high-flying Jackaroo, including the 05 Brock car, the dust would make life outrageously difficult ...

The Darwin of today is far different to the city I saw during the Repco Trial in 1979. Back then, Darwin was almost a frontier town. It was relatively new, having been almost totally rebuilt from the ground up after the devastation of Cyclone Tracy in December 1974.

Not that Darwin is no longer without its frontier town touches. Despite the tireless efforts of the wildlife rangers, crocodiles can regularly be spotted in Darwin's extensive harbour. This, of course, makes a trip to the beach to escape the heat a little tricky, while between October and March it's not advisable to take a dip in the ocean because of the number of box jellyfish in the area. The sting from a box jellyfish can be fatal. Thus, it is not surprising that most locals have chosen to put a pool in their backyard, rather than tempt fate with a day at the beach.

According to my brother Phil, however, except for the

dangers lurking in the sea, the lifestyle of Darwin is relaxed and the climate sensational. So it would have been nice to stay a while longer. Instead, though, we were headed to Tennant Creek, 1140 km and four special stages away.

Indeed this was to be the longest driving day of the rally, beginning at 5.30 am and ending over 12 hours later. Even at that time of the morning it was hot, so we ensured that there was an adequate supply of cold water in the esky. The competition would start with a special stage beginning 80 km outside the city.

Initially, the PlayStation was going to run east out of Darwin, entering Queensland via the Gulf town of Borroloola. This was the route we took in the '79 round-Australia. However, Mother Nature had put paid to those plans. Higher-than-average rainfall during the wet season had made parts of the gulf country almost completely impassable, so a hasty change in direction was required. Tennant Creek was chosen as the alternative destination.

The first stage was held in the rough and demanding hills near Rum Jungle, the site of the first uranium mine in the Northern Territory. The stage was short, but boy, it was tough. The track often followed a fence line and twisted and turned without warning, ducking and weaving over crests, sometimes running through dense jungle foliage and at other times on grass tracks that offered almost nothing in the way of traction.

Garland's dust! Being camped behind Bruce was a nightmare on the opening stage, as the dust he threw up in our faces made conditions intolerable at times. Until around 9.00 am there was no breeze at all to blow it away, or rain to wash the track clean. So there was no alternative in certain situations but to slow almost to a walk, 20 km/h maximum, because otherwise the dips, crests and bends in the track would have been impossible to recognise.

And the jungle looked so unforgiving. Still, the one thing you have to say about the conditions in the north of the Territory is that it offers plenty in the way of contrasts. After slipping and sliding through the jungle in the morning, with the canopy of trees keeping the dust at eyeline level, we discovered, 100 km down the road, that the second stage of the day presented a completely different challenge.

It was just 15 km long, but fast, open and wide—a rally (as opposed to off-road) driver's dream come true. The gravel was smooth but slippery in places; given the speeds achieved by the faster vehicles, a mistake might have meant an ambulance ride. For its part, our Jackaroo was absolutely flying, sliding around the long and open bends like a genuine rally car. We even ended up beating most of the 'real' rally cars, too; only the Commodores of Callinan and Wise got the better of our AMP 4 × 4. Not bad for a standard model.

A quick service at Emerald Springs and then we had a 400 km haul down the highway to the start of the next special stage, which would be held almost on the doorstep of one of the most famous pubs in the nation, the Daly Waters Hotel.

We raced along the transport stage as quickly as we dared, so that we would have time to stop at this national landmark. Just outside the pub stands what the locals claim is the most remote set of traffic lights in Australia. And they are always red! I reckon a lot of tourists must be aware of this oddity; judging by the busloads of people that were rolling in and out this is a 'must-see' place for everyone who travels to the Territory.

We had more than enough time for a couple of cold lemon squashes and a chat while sitting by the pool out the back of the pub. There was also enough time to talk to, and sign some autographs for, fellow patrons and take in the amazing amount of paraphernalia that lines just about every square centimetre of this most unique of Aussie institutions. These odds and ends range from an assortment of business cards pinned to the wall by travellers to, would you believe it, the earliest and latest in lingerie.

A few of the pub's patrons also took the time to jump into their vehicles to drive up to the start of the stage, just 700 m or so from the pub.

This 72 km run was held, for the most part, over smooth and fast station tracks. From about the halfway point, the route was overgrown with long grass, which made it difficult to determine exactly where the track was heading. The real trap was that the track was lined with anthills, some small but others absolutely huge, and there were even a few in the middle of the track. Believe me, they might have looked relatively harmless, but colliding with these things was like hitting solid concrete, and the low visbility meant that this was always a possibility. Unfortunately Keith Callinan and his co-driver, Paul Couper, could attest to their brutal nature, for they nailed an anthill big-time in their Commodore. Any chance they had of victory in the event came to a shuddering, shattering halt.

The next stage, which started at the Dunmarra Bore, 100 m off the Stuart Highway, was also no pushover. It was on this 95 km stage, which in parts was so fast and straight that I was wishing for another 100 horsepower and at least one more gear, that Ross Nicastri finally called it quits. The engine of his Jackaroo blew for the second time in the race and this time, rather than trying to fix it, he simply shipped the car back home and retired from the event.

It was sad to see Ross go, for he was one of the real characters of the event. He is also a bloke who knows how to drive at only one speed—flat out! I'd watched him in a few stages and could only marvel at how he managed to stay in control of a vehicle that was jumping, bucking and leaping skywards. In these circumstances, he kept his foot buried, even over the worst terrain imaginable. I was astounded at just how strong his Jackaroo was, to absorb so much punishment and keep coming back for more was remarkable.

But maybe we hadn't seen the last of him? As he said his goodbyes at the Tennant Creek service stop, after Day 11's racing was over, he intimated that he might fetch the family and rejoin the rally later in the event . . . as a spectator. Which, eventually, he did. Ironically, it would be Ross who would be on the spot when it all went wrong for us later in the rally. His help would be invaluable.

Aside from the long straights on this stage, which saw the Jackaroo regularly hitting 170 km/h (it may even have been going a bit faster), there were also areas where cattle on the route meant we had to thread our way cautiously along. The run to the finish line, however, was on an impediment-free 17 km-long straight over dried mudflats. There wasn't a pothole—nothing—to slow us down, just a shimmering horizon to aim at.

I grinned at Webby and asked, 'Windows wound up?'

'Yep.'

'No corners?'

'Nope.'

'Okay, we're here, let's see what this thing can do.'

I just held the pedal to the metal and went for it. Afterwards, we learned the Jackaroo had been the fastest car on the road— it sure could motor when we asked it to.

DAY 12

TENNANT CREEK
TO
CLONCURRY

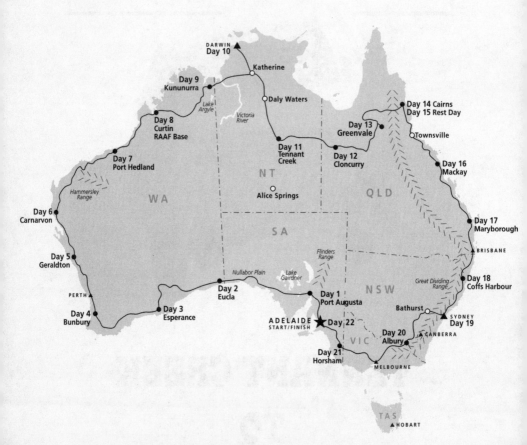

DARWIN
Day 10

Katherine

Day 9
Kununurra

Lake
Argyle

Day 8
Curtin
RAAF Base

Victoria
River

Daly Waters

Day 14 Cairns
Day 15 Rest Day

Townsville

Day 13
Greenvale

Day 7
Port Hedland

Day 11
Tennant
Creek

Day 12
Cloncurry

Day 16
Mackay

Hammersley
Range

N T

W A

Alice Springs

Q L D

Day 6
Carnarvon

S A

Day 17
Maryborough

Day 5
Geraldton

Flinders
Range

BRISBANE

PERTH

Nullabor Plain

Lake
Gairdner

Day 2
Eucla

Day 1
Port Augusta

Great Dividing
Range

Day 18
Coffs Harbour

N S W

Day 4
Bunbury

Day 3
Esperance

Bathurst

SYDNEY
Day 19

ADELAIDE
START/FINISH

Day 22

CANBERRA

Day 20
Albury

V I C

Day 21
Horsham

MELBOURNE

TAS

HOBART

T he real surprise packet of the rally was the Datsun 180B SSS driven by the New South Wales pair of Rob Gambino and David Lowe. By the end of Day 12, despite the fact that their engine was half the size of the monsters still in front of them, they were up to seventh place, and climbing.

The sixth-placed Jackaroo of Queenslanders Peter Lockhart and Tim Donovan was firmly in their sights, less than two minutes ahead. Even the fourth and fifth-placed cars, Warren and Joy Ridge in the 1993 Mitsubishi Pajero and Reg Owen and Russell Cairns in the 1998 Nissan Patrol, were looking anxiously over their shoulders.

This was going to be a long day dominated by transport stages. Apart from two special stages, both in the Territory, it was basically nothing more than a run to Cloncurry, situated about 100 km east of Mount Isa in north-west Queensland.

Many of the adventures scheduled for the day became casualties of the gulf country's big wet. Organisers were forced to bypass the area where the rally was originally going to head and find alternative routes—and that meant losing a few of the planned stages. In fact, one of the stages planned for just north of Mt Isa was destroyed, leaving two 'competitives'—one 88 km and the other 110 km—and then the long haul along the highway.

The first section of the day, an 88 km run through land owned by the Waramungu, Mungkarta and Wakaya people, contained enough thrills on its own. This Aboriginal land is normally off-limits to the general public. In fact, the PlayStation Rally was only the second event ever granted permission to use it (the other was the Australian Safari).

Over the years, Bob Carpenter has developed a close relationship with a great number of Aboriginal communities, which has allowed him to gain access to their land. He knows the people, and he knows their roads. Without their permission we would have been obliged to spend many more, less interesting hours on the bitumen. It meant, though, that we had to observe certain procedures precisely, in return for the Aboriginal land owners' support. If we were told to close a gate after we went through, then we did. If we were asked to observe a quiet zone through part of the stage, then we did. No questions asked; we were visitors and we did as we were told, just as we had done when rallying through the huge stations of Western Australia.

The stage started off on fast, wide roads, but quickly entered country where the tracks were seldom, if ever, graded and where there were some huge washaways. Several times we were obliged to detour around absolutely enormous holes in the middle of the track. If we'd careered off into one of these caverns, I kid you not, the following competitors would have been able to use the roof of the Jackaroo as part of the road. Yes, they were *that* deep.

The second stage, in total contrast, was incredibly fast. In fact, for the entire 110 km, Webby had just nine calls to make and not one was a turn; it was either straight on or keep left. At one stage there was a 53 km gap between instructions, the Jackaroo hammering away at top speed while, much to my amazement, my co-driver . . . fell asleep. True, he actually nodded off.

Sure, there were a few fast corners that could easily catch out the unwary, but aside from some trickier stuff towards the end, a fast time on this stage required little more than a heap of horsepower and the ability to keep the vehicle in a straight line.

It took us just 45 minutes to put the 110 km of dirt behind us. That time, if nothing else, is a good indication of just how long we were at full speed.

From the conclusion of the stage, it was just a 10 km hop down to the Barkly Roadhouse for a quick service and then a 570 km transport haul to Cloncurry.

At Barkly we ran into a busload of tourists and the scene quickly erupted into a photo shoot, with just about every passenger seeking a happy snap.

We left the roadhouse and 247 km later, we crossed the cattle grid that divides the Northern Territory and Queensland. First stop in the sunshine state was Mt Isa, where the organisers had set up a passage control—a checkpoint that ensures everyone travels along the set course—at the Mobil service station on the outskirts of town. It was here that a local TV crew caught up with us for a quick interview for the regional stations.

Media commitments over, we grabbed Bruce Garland and Harry Suzuki, who were also parked at the servo, and made a committee decision to explore the immediate vicinity in search of a quick bite to eat.

Out onto the main road, down a cross street, a quick turnaround, then down another street and we discovered a little takeaway shop, where Bruce, Harry and Webby ordered hamburgers and I grabbed a sandwich. We were just starting our meal when a woman rushed through the door and up to our table. She was almost in tears, fighting to regain her breath so she could speak.

'I'm from the Holden dealership,' she gasped, 'just down the road. I saw your Jackaroos chuck a U-turn, and thought you were leaving. Can I just ask you guys for a photo with the cars?'

The poor girl had put in a very long sprint, desperate to catch us before we left town.

'Not a problem,' Bruce and I said in unison. 'Just give us a chance to finish our lunch,' I continued, 'and we'll pop up and say G'day.'

When we got there, I reckon I had my photo taken with every employee in the place and signed every scrap of Holden Racing Team and Holden material they could lay their hands on. It is always fantastic to meet people who are so enthusiastic.

And speaking of enthusiastic, while in Mount Isa we also ran into a very keen Brock fan, who stopped to have a photo taken with me and his truck. He was driving the vehicle for the North Queensland Fire Safety Services, but what struck me was the number plate his truck was carrying . . . FSS 05.

Then, in Cloncurry, we met a couple who owned one of the original modified Commodore SL/Es we had manufactured for HDT Special Vehicles back in 1981. We only made 500 of that model, and to find one of them in pristine condition, 17 years later . . . in Cloncurry! I always thought of that vehicle as a 'city' type of car, never saw it as something you'd see meandering down the main street of a town in north-west Queensland. And that car's number plate?

HDT 01.

DAY 13

CLONCURRY
TO
GREENVALE

'H igh-speed chess' is how an ebullient David Lowe described the PlayStation after Day 13. He was echoing some earlier comments by Clerk of the Course Bob Carpenter, who had often called the rally a 'thinking person's event'.

In one day Lowe and his partner Rob Gambino had climbed from seventh to fifth place, and were within eight seconds of the fourth-placed Nissan Patrol of Reg Owen and Russell Cairns. In fact, 11 seconds now covered the fourth, fifth and sixth cars. That sixth spot belonged to Peter Lockhart and Tim Donovan's Jackaroo.

Lowe was once a driver of Mini Coopers and Ford Cortinas on the Australian motor racing scene, and then Formula Fords in the UK, before disappearing from the scene after he went to live in the United States. He returned to Australia in 1996. Gambino, a high school mathematics teacher, estimated that he had rebuilt the Datsun in around three months leading into the PlayStation.

'We wanted to build it light,' explained Lowe. 'That, to us, is the key.'

Having survived the terrors of Western Australia in one piece, third place was now a realistic goal. 'Rob has not put a foot wrong,' Lowe said, 'he's driving extraordinarily well.

'We'll be turning the wick up.'

Bob Carpenter had done sensationally well at locating and gaining permission to use some of the most challenging rally tracks in the nation, but not even he could conjure something out of nothing. Which is why we faced a 290 km transport stage along the Flinders Highway, which bisects the north-west tablelands of Queensland, before reaching our first competitive stage of the day. The geography out of Cloncurry is flat, and while the black soil plains are perfect for raising cattle, they're not much chop for rallying.

And so we faced a long run down the blacktop to the township of Richmond, where the local Apex Club was waiting to greet us opposite our refuelling point. They had put together an impressive spread, offering free tea and coffee as well as cakes, pies and sausage sandwiches for those who didn't mind handing over a couple of dollars.

From our point of view, it was an opportune stop for another reason as well. We had discovered on the run from Cloncurry to Richmond that our in-car intercom system, which allows us to talk to each other on special stages when otherwise the clatter would make communication impossible, had given up the ghost. Fortunately, our crew carried a spare unit, and we used the 15 minutes available to have it fitted.

The opening stage of the day was a 170 km monster that, according to the notes, would be the most varied of the entire rally, offering at least a little bit of everything, including sand, gravel, rocks and bitumen. We started the stage over a flat river plain, complete with plenty of cattle grids that could be attacked almost flat-out.

As I've explained, I'd discovered early in the event that the Jackaroo was quicker, under certain conditions, in two-wheel drive. This was especially true on the smoother rally roads such as this one. However, during this first stage of Day 13, we entered a long left-hand bend that, ever tightening, led into a cattle grid. For a moment, I thought we might be in deep trouble, because without four-wheel drive it would inevitably take longer to correct the slide we were in, and hitting the right-hand side of the grid seemed a distinct possibility. Such a collision would have been a total disaster.

Alternatively, we could have continued to the right of the grid—a thought that crossed my mind when I first realised the predicament the car was in—but had I detoured in this way, we would have fallen into a severe washaway from which there was no escape. Instead, I jerked the wheel hard and, as the Jackaroo straightened, I thought we'd sneak through. The ripping sounds that came after the right-hand front of the car clipped the metal stanchions at the side of the grid suggested otherwise.

Clunk! The Jackaroo gave a bit of a jolt, but we were still on the road. We pulled over to the side of the track and leapt out, to find there was not a mark on the car, but that the front right tyre had been torn to shreds. We were in the process of changing it when Bruce roared past.

We could hear him call over the radio, 'Roadside assist? Not today!' followed by some maniacal laughter. Endurance rallying charity doesn't extend to changing tyres. But after our rehearsal back on day three, our first day in Western Australia, this tyre change went smoothly, and within a few minutes we were back in the Jackaroo and on our way, thanking our lucky stars.

Looking back, we realised that the impact of the accident was so severe that, had we been in a conventional race car, the front suspension would have been ripped clean out and we would have been dead and buried.

As it was, we'd only had to replace a tyre and we were back on the road. Well, for a few hundred metres, at least. We'd only been back on the road for a couple of minutes when the rear tyre, which had also obviously been damaged in the altercation with the grid, decided to give up the ghost. It blew big-time, so yet again, we had to pull over to the side of the road and fit a spare.

From this point, we needed to be careful to look after the tyres, for the only tyres we now had on board, apart from the four on the road, had been wrecked. This was a little disconcerting, for there was still something like 140 km of rallying to complete and the roads would get much tougher before the end of the day, with lots of creek crossings, rocky patches and grids between us and the finish. Unfortunately there were also a fair few closed gates for Webby to handle, which is just what he felt like after being involved in two tyre changes in double-quick time.

Fortunately, the service point following this stage was less than four km down the road, in the enthusiastic little town of Hughenden. Bob Carpenter had been required to get the approval of more than 40 land owners in order to close roads and run the two stages in this area. That support was evident by the reception we received in this township of 2000 plus. The kids had been given time off school to see the rally arrive, which created a real carnival atmosphere as we rolled into town. At one point, I borrowed a young bloke's pushbike and took another little kid for a dink along the main road.

Around 70 km north of Hughenden, you'll find Porcupine Gorge, which the locals like to call North Queensland's Grand Canyon. It's a most spectacular sight and, after our 30-minute service stop, that's where we headed for the start of the second special stage. We'd be beginning just one km away from the rim of this stunning natural wonder.

The second stage was 58 km long. Aside from some unwary cattle and a collection of rough creek crossings, it presented few problems and we emerged unscathed for the long haul to our overnight stop in the little township of Greenvale.

And a long and incredibly dusty trip it was too. Even on a well-maintained dirt road, the amount of dust created by the vehicles in front was staggering, reducing visibility to virtually nil. This resulted in a nasty tangle that left one of our Jackaroo service vehicles sitting shattered by the roadside. The crash occurred about 90 km into the transport stage, just after a dry creek crossing. Bruce Garland's team manager, Nigel Bolling, had been driving and had ducked out to overtake a slower vehicle, only to discover a monster road train travelling at walking pace through the dip. The Jackaroo slammed into the back of the road train, which didn't even feel the impact and continued on its way. Our car, however, was mortally wounded and those inside considerably worse off for the experience.

Nigel had cut his hand pretty badly, while one of the mechanics had really hurt his legs and was in considerable pain. Not much later, Bruce Garland arrived and then our giant Isuzu service truck was at the scene.

Then thankfully, the Repsol representitives in their massive Holden Suburban came along to take the injured crew members away in air-conditioned comfort. Meanwhile, the rest of the crew attempted to revive the shattered Jackaroo so that it could at least complete the haul down to Greenvale.

Somehow, using plenty of bush engineering expertise, they did it, and a vehicle I reckoned had been close to a write-off not only made it to the end of the day, but kept on going for the rest of the rally. The Jackaroo might have been cosmetically challenged, but it was up and running—the ingenuity of Garland's crew was something to behold and I was glad they were on our side. Their innovative repair techniques included, for example, holding the radiator in place with a plastic zip-tie. In an event such as this, the ability to improvise on the spot can often mean the difference between winning and losing, or of finishing or being stranded out in the middle of nowhere.

The service crews are outrageously resourceful, nothing fazes them. This attitude extends to most of the drivers too. They live for the sport and the challenges it throws up. 'You've got to keep the show on the road' is their attitude and I've seen countless examples in endurance events of innovative thinking from experts who can adapt their vast knowledge of cars to any situation.

I remember a classic example from 1995. During one special stage, I had an altercation with another car. It had slowed to let me pass but, at the very last moment, instead of pulling off the road, it slid and blocked my way through. With nowhere to go, I hit its back corner and the front of my Commodore folded up like tissue paper.

I needed a tow, and a bloke came along in a four-door, four-wheel drive Rodeo ute to help. At this point, we were about 20 km from the end of the stage, and for the next few kilomteres the track got progressively worse. The road had broken through the top surface, so we were deep in mud. Conditions deteriorated to such a degree that the guy who was towing me couldn't get me any further.

What to do? My radiator was shot, so while I could still start and run the car I only had a limited time to do it in or I'd risk overheating the engine. Up above us, a few metres away from and about two metres higher than the road, was a railway line. This my accomplice decided was the way clear.

But I was bogged rotten.

'Have you got a snatch strap?' he asked.

'Yeah,' I replied.

'Let's have a look at it.'

He took my snatch strap—a long, very strong strap—and joined it to his. Then he linked his car to one end of this elongated rubber band, and my car to the other end. Then he jumped back in his ute and four-wheel drove up onto the railway track, parking back behind me and to my left as I sat in my driver's seat, pointing straight ahead. I fired my engine up ...

He said 'Go!' I put the Commodore into first gear, and he shot past, absolutely flat out, and pulled me out like a plug out of the bath. Next thing, I'm doing 40 km up on the top of the rise, straight behind him, and enjoying the best ride I think I have ever had in a motor car. The tea-trees around us got flattened a bit, but it was just fantastic. A minute earlier I thought I was stuck in that mud heap forever.

As I've explained, this sort of thing happens in off-road racing. Your rivals will come around and help you out, using their experience, instinct and initiative to solve dilemmas that at first glance seemed event-ending. I have seen cars in rallies with a winch cable lassoing the chassis—from the front bumper bar, over the windscreen, the roof, the boot and underneath— to keep it together until the next service stop. It is amazing how you can actually accomplish a lot of things if you stop to think about it. Too many people give up too easily. This is why an event such as the PlayStation can be such a fantastic character-building exercise.

One of the major attractions of Greenvale is the Three Rivers Hotel, which was made famous by the song first performed by country legend Stan Costa. My favourite version of the song, however, is the one by John Williamson, and I made the point of putting the tape on and singing along as we headed into town.

The people of Greenvale enthusiastically welcomed the rally, the local school kids coming out and offering to wash the rally vehicles for the bargain price of five dollars. Of course, the kids were little and the Jackaroo big, so both Webby and

I had to pitch in and help anyway, but having the locals involved added to the fun.

The only place to be that night was in the Three Rivers Hotel, which put on a fabulous meal for all the crews. I also took the chance to catch up with Des West, a racing legend as far as I'm concerned, as he celebrated his 70th birthday. Dessie and I shared a Monaro in the 1969 Bathurst race. Back then, I was very much the new kid on the block and he was the established ace.

The 1969 Bathurst was, of course, most memorable for the incredible accident that happened when Bill Brown rolled his Falcon and started a chain reaction which ultimately claimed a quarter of the field. Here was I, having my first run at the mountain, and pretty wide-eyed. In contrast, Des was probably the most relaxed and laid-back driver I had ever met, then or now. What a character! He'd been racing Holdens since the 1950s and, when things got boring during his stint, he reckoned that he'd light up a cigarette while heading down Conrod— even back then the old, 350 cubic inch Monaro was hitting something like 210 km/h. Imagine doing something like that now?

We ended up finishing third in that race, on the same lap and pretty close behind the winner, my old mate Colin Bond, in another of the Holden Dealer Team Monaros. Unfortunately for Bondy, it would be his one and only triumph at Bathurst. Certainly, he deserved more, for he was one of the best drivers Australia has ever produced.

DAY 14

GREENVALE
TO
CAIRNS

From now on, the rally would enter a new phase, as the harsh and dusty conditions of the outback were replaced by the smoother, more slippery roads through the forests of the east coast. With the change of scenery and climate would come a new set of conditions to challenge the PlayStation field. The field was now leaving the Queensland plains and heading back into the hills. Most of the day's rallying would be held in the tablelands that mark the northern edge of the Great Dividing Range, the 'backbone of the nation' that runs all the way, parallel with the coast, to Victoria.

Before the cars and crews left the Three Rivers Hotel behind, they had around 840 km to travel before reaching the coast at Cairns. The five stages scheduled for the day were all relatively short, sharp special stages which would be run over smooth gravel roads.

At this point in the rally the advantage would start to swing away from the four-wheel drives and back in favour of the faster and more nimble rally cars. For the best part of two weeks the rally had been pounding its way through some of the most remote and isolated places in the nation. It had been a hard, uncompromising slog. Sometimes the field had followed little more than a couple of barely discernable wheel tracks, and there was no denying that in such conditions the big four-wheel drives, with their tough chassis construction, high ground clearance, extended wheel travel and amazing traction, had held all the cards. Outback rallying was where the four-wheel drives were expected to excel, and they had.

Consequently, by the time the field departed Greenvale, four-wheel drives had four of the first five places firmly nailed down. Bruce Garland continued to hold a commanding lead in his Jackaroo, the Brock Jackaroo was second, while Reg Owen was fourth, just in front of Peter Lockhart in yet another

Jackaroo and the Datsun 180B of David Lowe and Rob Gambino in fifth place.

The exceptionally well-driven Commodore ute of Graeme Wise was proving to be the wild card in the leading pack. Wise had worked his way into a position where, now that the roads were about to swing back in the favour of the cars, he could mount a very serious challenge.

But every driver had to be careful. 'We've noticed,' remarked David Lowe, 'that once people start going backwards, it's very hard to reverse the trend.'

Bruce Garland and I had established a hefty lead on those in pursuit, but there was still plenty of time and distance remaining for Graeme Wise, who had definitely been setting himself up for a charge, to eat away at our hard-won advantage. Perhaps our best hope lay in the fact that Bob Carpenter was hinting that although the run down the east coast would definitely be easier than some of the gut-wrenching stuff we'd encountered, it would be a long way from a stroll.

There would, he promised with a sly grin, still be something for everyone—cars and four-wheel drives.

Continuing its move up the field was that most unlikely of round-Australia vehicles, the 1973 Datsun 180B SSS driven by Rob Gambino with David Lowe navigating. Gambino was proving to be a smart operator, for he knew when to charge and when to take things easy.

The quietly-spoken Gambino and the extroverted Lowe had rebuilt this old rally car from the ground up. They were followed by a service crew of just three, which included Rob's girlfriend and David's wife, but were embarrassing some of the bigger budget operations with their car's performance. This was truly a case of David taking on Goliath. While no one in the PlayStation enjoyed a massive budget, these guys were operating on the proverbial shoestring yet doing a brilliant job. At some stages, they even found it almost impossible to source tyres for their car. Having worked their way up from 22nd on the opening day, they were, at this stage, motoring along in fifth place and making time on those in front.

Lowe, a genuine character, kept warning those ahead, 'We're comin' to get you!' I don't think he was joking. Certainly, if Gambino kept driving with the verve and cleverness he had been showing, this unlikely combination could well have the means to upset some of the big guns. Could you imagine ... a 1973 Datsun winning the PlayStation Rally Round Australia 1998?

The first four stages of Day 14 were smooth and very fast, although there were places where the rough conditions— especially some of the creek crossings and washaways—would have slowed the rally cars down a little. The final stage of the day was similar, except it contained one trap for young players ...

A 50-metre long concrete causeway, located over a crest just after a tight left-hand bend, did prove to be something of an eye-opener. On the approach we saw a large posse of spectators perched on a hill, who would only have been there if they were anticipating some action below, so we should have been ready. If there's one thing I've learned over the years about rallying it's that spectators don't assemble where there's no chance of something happening. Rally enthusiasts have an unerring ability to find the spots where there's a prospect of disaster occurring, and in this instance they picked a good place. With the crest camouflaging the impending danger, there was a good chance that, after sliding through the bend, a vehicle would find itself on the causeway before it could get back in a straight line. No way was the causeway wide enough to be driven over sideways!

We made it, but only by the skin of our teeth. For the fans, it must have looked as if we got it exactly right. We couldn't have gone over any faster. I knew now why the rally instructions had given a 'triple caution', the ultimate warning. As Bob Carpenter had pointed out in his pre-rally briefing: 'If you hit a single (caution), you'll have a bingle; hit a double, you'll be in big trouble; hit a triple and you'll end up a cripple'. This may have been taking things to an extreme, but I reflected on his words now.

The causeway was narrow, fell sharply from the left-hand side, and there were huge boulders on either side. And the left-hand edge is exactly where Bruce ended up. The skid marks he left on the causeway told part of the story; fans who saw his misadventure described later how he miscued his entry onto the causeway by less than a metre. The Jackaroo almost fell off the edge, but ground its way across, half on and half off the concrete crossing, on the engine skid plate. A number of onlookers—and Bruce, too!—raved about the shower of sparks. Fortunately for him, this slip-up caused no major damage.

One vehicle that didn't escape unscathed was the third-placed Commodore ute. In an incident that could have cost him the chance to challenge the leaders, Graeme Wise suffered a puncture, but without a spare, was obliged to drive on to the end of the stage, 12 km away. It seems he'd damaged his rear axle, and might have to take things a bit easy.

However, Graeme remained positive. 'No worries,' he said

to me. 'It'll be extremely difficult for us to catch you, but we'll give it a shot.'

There remained only one more service stop, at Atherton, before we headed into Cairns. As usual a crowd quickly gathered around 05, and in their midst was one of my cousins, who, I have to admit, I hadn't seen since the Repco Trial came through here in 1979. And herein lies a tale . . .

In 1979, I was in Atherton, waiting to start a special stage, when this very attractive young lady came up to me, wished me luck and gave me a peck on the cheek. Then off I went, fast as I could, to the end of the stage. And something extraordinary happened. There was the very same girl, only this time she congratulated me on my performance before giving me another kiss. But how did she get there before me? It wasn't possible. Couldn't be.

Identical twins! These two girls were, in fact, distant cousins of mine, and they'd set me up in the nicest possible way. Now, 19 years later, they repeated the stunt. While the element of surprise was missing, it was as good to see them again as it had been to meet them the first time. And when we recalled that day 19 years before, we laughed as loudly and as long as we had done when the prank was first played out.

Unfortunately, as was the case almost two decades earlier, we didn't have long to catch up on family matters, as the stop was only for 15 minutes.

Speaking of family matters, I really was looking forward to getting to Cairns, for the following day was the rally's scheduled rest day. Bev and my daughter, Alexandra, were flying up to spend some time; in fact, Bev was planning to spend a few days in Cairns.

DAY 15

REST DAY
(CAIRNS)

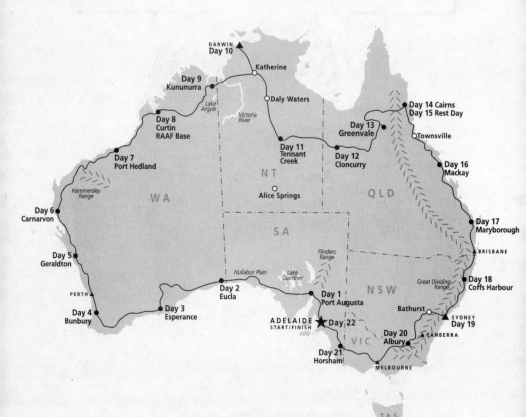

DARWIN
Day 10

Katherine

Lake
Argyle

Day 9
Kununurra

Daly Waters

Day 8
Curtin
RAAF Base

Victoria
River

Day 13
Greenvale

Day 14 Cairns
Day 15 Rest Day

Townsville

Day 7
Port Hedland

Day 11
Tennant
Creek

Day 12
Cloncurry

Day 16
Mackay

Hammersley
Range

N T

W A

Alice Springs

Q L D

Day 6
Carnarvon

S A

Day 17
Maryborough

Day 5
Geraldton

Flinders
Range

BRISBANE

Nullabor Plain

Lake
Gairdner

Great Dividing
Range

Day 18
Coffs Harbour

PERTH

Day 2
Eucla

Day 1
Port Augusta

N S W

Bathurst

Day 3
Esperance

SYDNEY
Day 19

Day 4
Bunbury

ADELAIDE
START/FINISH

Day 22

CANBERRA

Day 20
Albury

V I C

Day 21
Horsham

MELBOURNE

T A S

HOBART

J ust to prove that no sporting event can ever be free of controversy, a couple of competitors at the back of the field questioned whether the 05 Jackaroo met the rules of the event, their protest specifically targeting the car's fuel filler arrangements. The point of concern was that the filler allowed the use of leaded petrol and, given that it was a 1998 model vehicle, this was outside Australian design rules.

There's a lot of differences between a road vehicle and one built to undertake an off-road rally. Safety is a key concern in an event such as this, which is why fuel tanks approved by the FIA (the controlling body of world motorsport)—in the case of the Jackaroo, a 160-litre tank mounted on the rear floor—are required. These tanks are specifically designed for a worst-case scenario: if you're involved in a crash, the last thing you want is fuel pouring out of a ruptured tank. Fire is a potential danger that concerns every competitive driver, for such is the construction of modern vehicles that there's a very good chance of surviving even the most horrific accident. But without quick intervention—and when you're in the middle of the bush there are no fire crews to rush to the scene like on a racing circuit—a fire can take a life very quickly. The tank in Brock's Jackaroo had been declared legal at pre-event scrutineering, so many observers couldn't see a problem.

A two-hour hearing took place and the protest was, as expected, dismissed.

Frankly, I wasn't interested in the protest. The case needed to go before the stewards of the event, which meant that the team had to present a defence against the charges. I left this in the hands of Bruce Garland, team manager, Nigel Bolling and Webby.

I was more concerned about enjoying the day with my family. I once had a holiday place in Cairns. For years I had an old Holden station wagon sitting up there so we had transport whenever we could get away for a few days. That old wagon was pretty beat up, the back was full of junk and we never even locked it because frankly, we knew no one would bother to steal it. I think it just rusted away eventually.

Of course, it's not hard to see why Cairns is one of the most popular tourist spots in the nation. The climate is superb, the scenery spectacular and it is very much the gateway to the extraordinary delights of the Great Barrier Reef. Each and every day, boats of various sizes pull out of Cairns Harbour for a day on the reef, giving tourists the chance to snorkel and dive in one of the natural wonders of the world. A trip to the reef was on my list of things to do. I had arranged to go out on a boat to try a little scuba diving and Alexandra was keen to try it as well.

While I was looking forward to a day off, our crew would be hard at work. The constant pounding that had been handed out to the Jackaroo was starting to take its toll. The front chassis had started to bend outwards quite alarmingly and stress fractures were beginning to appear. It was a problem that needed to be nipped in the bud, for if the chassis kept on bending, the engine, quite literally, would fall out. That, at least, was the worst-case scenerio. The boys planned to take the Jackaroo out of parc ferme and down to the local Holden dealer, where the engine would be removed, and the front chassis welded and realigned.

While the organisers had given the crews an extended period on the rest day to revive the cars, this didn't mean they had all day to work on the Jackaroo. In fact, every minute was critical, to the point that I had made sure to fill up with petrol the night before. Thus, the crew wouldn't have to waste a couple of minutes doing so the following day.

Away from the rally, I had a great day, although I did have to be back at the hotel in the early afternoon to have my photo taken with a politician from my electorate back in Victoria. She was standing for the upcoming Federal elections and reckoned that a photo with me would help win a few votes. She was so keen to get the picture that she actually flew up from Melbourne with a photographer in the morning and was heading back in the afternoon.

Now I don't want to get involved in politics, and I won't endorse any one side or the other, but I was happy to say that she was a good woman who would do a good job if elected so I was glad to have my photo taken with her.

Over the years many people have approached me to get involved in politics. In fact, I've been approached by both major parties with the view of standing for election myself, but it's something I have no problem in rejecting.

I feel that I can achieve more by staying out of the political arena, for that gives me the chance to lobby whatever side is in power about things that really concern me, especially road safety matters. I reckon it's better to stay on the outside looking in; because I have no ties with either side I am able to talk with both. Thankfully, having a high profile allows me access to politicians and I have the opportunity to push for things I see as really important such as improved driver training.

It stands to reason that if we teach people to drive better, the accident rate will fall, but you'd be amazed at how hard it is to get that message across to the decision-makers.

DAY 16

CAIRNS
TO
MACKAY

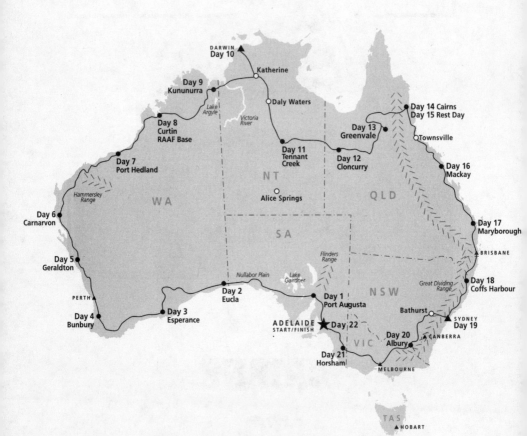

Day 16 fell on Reg Owen's 53rd birthday. By the end of the day's racing, two over-50s—Brock was the other—were in second and third place, chasing the young buck, 40-year-old Bruce Garland.

Before the day began, Owen received a birthday gift from home. His wife, Jenny, had sent him a map of Australia and a compass . . . so he could find his way home!

Owen's other birthday present came in the shape of a major setback for the Commodore ute of Graeme Wise and Linda Long. Having been as low as 14th early on, the ute had reached the top three without passing a car. The strategy was simple: 'We're just keeping out of mischief,' Russell Cairns told a reporter from their proud local paper, the *Warrnambool Standard*, 'the cars in front have all had problems or broken down'.

David Lowe and Rob Gambino were back in the top four, and continuing their battle with the Jackaroo of Lockhart and Donovan. A mere 34 seconds separated the two cars.

The rest day at the Novotel Palms Resort in Cairns proved too much for the 1966 Morris Mini Cooper S team of Doug Coote and Cono Onofaro. They missed the start of Day 16 after sleeping in, and then withdrew for the day. They had persisted despite numerous problems, spending 16 nights in a row fixing first one problem and then another. A sheared steering bolt, which caused the Mini to crash into two trees, was the final straw.

Though battered, they intended to repair their car in the morning, and then get it down to Mackay by the end of the day, so these brave warriors and their gallant vehicle could rejoin the event in time for the run to Maryborough.

We had an early start from Cairns. The first vehicle was due away at 4.00 am, which is probably why Bev decided to say goodbye to me as I left the room rather than coming to see me off at the start. In fact, I thought I was going to have to continue by myself, for as I walked to the vehicle in the darkness, there was no sign of my co-driver. Luckily he wasn't far away, it's just that he was moving slowly in the early hours of the morning.

Not that he really needed to be on the ball from the word go, for the opening leg of the day was a 315 km run down the bitumen before we reached the first competitive stage.

It was around mid-morning when we rolled into our first service stop at Townsville, a little earlier than expected after the second stage of the day was cancelled.

The scheduled 25 km run through rainforest had certainly sounded like a lot of fun, the road having only recently been repaired after being badly damaged the previous wet season. Unfortunately, it seemed they would be repairing it again, for flooding in the Townsville area just before we arrived had not only again made the road virtually impassable, but had washed away a bridge.

Not that it was hard to imagine, for the opening stage of the day—a 34 km section—had been run in heavy rain and the road surface alternated between gravel and slippery clay. This was a real test of a driver's ability to read the conditions and adjust speed appropriately. Even with the advantage of four-wheel drive, sometimes the Jackaroo was fighting and scrambling for grip on a surface that would have been hard to walk along without losing your footing. One thing was certain, the guys in the two-wheel drive vehicles would have been finding out just what oversteer was all about.

The transport stage down into Townsville was almost just

as interesting as a special stage. The road that runs from the mountains where the township of Paluma can be found, contains one section where there are 230 bends—no, we didn't count them but someone who did told us—in just 17 km of bitumen. It is, indeed, a long and winding road.

After a 30-minute service and publicity break in Townsville, it was then on to the next stage, which started on the Kirknie Station. A number of locals had turned up for a chat and to grab some pictures, and because we arrived early there was a good chance to have a talk with the station owners. They bemoaned the effects of the dry weather—despite the fact that, less than 200 km back up the road the locals there had been complaining about the floods!

How tough is it on the land these days? Those who live and work on the land are the real backbone of the nation. They lead a way of life that often doesn't provide the just rewards for the effort they put in.

Not too long into the special stage, the route notes warned drivers to take special care making a rather tricky right turn; despite the warning we made an error. We turned right just before a creek crossing, only to find later that the correct turn came *after* the creek crossing rather than before it. Instead of crossing the creek and then making the turn, we were caught out by a guy sitting on the bonnet of a four-wheel drive at the edge of the track, waving his arm. It looked like he was telling us where to go, and we accepted his lead. Off we went, barnstorming along the road until we came to a fence and a gate. There was no mention of the gate in the route book, but we were still certain we were on the right track.

Webby leapt out of the Jackaroo and raced to the gate, only to be confronted with a typical North Queensland affair constructed from several strands of evil-looking barbed wire tied to a couple of large tree branches. The locking mechanism of these things is, for city dwellers, very sinister.

Webby stood there, totally baffled. With the clock ticking, I was screaming and yelling at him to open the thing. Given that I'm no stranger to the country, I could see how simple it was. All he needed to do was slide a loop of wire along the branch, which was holding the fence in place, and it would open. Webby tried everything: pushing, pulling, yanking, yelling and, by now, bleeding.

As he struggled with the fence, the barbed wire had cut into his hand. It was a bit of a mess by the time I got out to help. I got the gate open in a couple of seconds, rushed back to the Jackaroo and drove through. Now Webby couldn't close the gate, but as I revved the engine the prospect of being left behind convinced him to redouble his efforts and, while it probably wasn't shut in the manner in which it had been designed, at least it was closed.

Frustrated at losing so much time, I went pounding down the track while Webby fumbled with his route chart and bled all over the place. I told him flatly to forget about the cut until the end of the stage. We could do something about it then.

We'd probably travelled a kilometre or so down this track when Webby yelled for me to stop. The course we were on didn't correlate with the notes he had in front of him and he was now convinced that we'd taken a wrong turn somewhere. The best thing to do in these circumstances was to backtrack until we picked up the right trail. I wasn't so sure, but he had the book and I was in his hands. So around we went.

Back to the gate!

The second time around was little better than the first, but Webby did eventually get it down and then back up, again not in the approved FNQ style. It would hold okay, we figured, until someone could come back to secure it properly. We finally got back to the place where we'd turned right, and this time the guy who had waved us down the wrong road was running towards us, to show us the correct route. What we had taken as a wave to turn right had, it seemed, been nothing but a friendly greeting. You live and learn.

We reckon we'd dropped something like four of five minutes by exploring a part of the bush where we were never meant to be, which meant that we'd probably dropped a few places down the field, but it wasn't a total disaster.

We'd only gone a few hundred metres down the track when we saw the white Pedders ute of Wise and Long parked at the side of the track. Both were out of the vehicle and had removed their helmets, which indicated a major problem. It transpired that Graeme had clouted a hefty rock on a creek crossing, the one which we had missed initially, and holed his sump. After all the effort he had put in to climbing up to third place, it was a sad ending to his chances in the event.

As we passed them, I noticed Wise was walking back up the track, searching for something. When I asked him later what he was after, he laughed a little, and explained, 'I was hunting for the rock that got us. I wanted it as a souvenir'.

Fired up by our miscue, I was pressing on as hard as I dared, and we started catching and passing the vehicles that had snuck by while we were off the track. We caught up to Mark Griffith's little RAV4 about 10 km from the end, but were trapped in his dust. This is what I call 'bulldust country'. When the cars churn through, the very black soil evolves into very black dust that gets into everything: your car, shoes, clothes, mouth, eyes, even under your armpits. Everywhere. Not pleasant, or easy to drive through. Webby grabbed the radio to let Mark know we were on his tail. And he called and he called. Eventually, as we were rocketing up a steep hill, a voice came over the radio ...

'Car 14 [Griffith] ... 05 is right behind you. Move over.'

Where did that come from? Bob Carpenter was standing at the top of the hill, saw what was happening and decided to offer his advice to Mark. This did the trick and we roared on past and headed to the end of the stage.

That night in Mackay, Webby sought the medical attention of Geoff Becker, who reckoned the cut wouldn't need stitches and taped it up. But the doctor was keen to give him a tetanus injection. This was not a prospect that was greeted with much enthusiasm by the patient, for tetanus injections hurt like hell, which is probably why Geoff was so keen to give it in the first place.

At that night's service stop, inside the Mackay showgrounds, the decision was taken to replace both the clutch and gearbox of our Jackaroo. Bruce Garland admitted he had little experience with the longevity of the standard clutch plate that we were using in our unmodified Jackaroo, but reasoned that it paid to be safe rather than sorry. The new gearbox would be installed for the same reason. 'We've got a spare,' Bruce argued, 'so we may as well use it.'

As it was, when the clutch was removed it looked close to brand new. At least we knew that the newly-installed one would easily carry us back to Adelaide.

DAY 17

MACKAY
TO
MARYBOROUGH

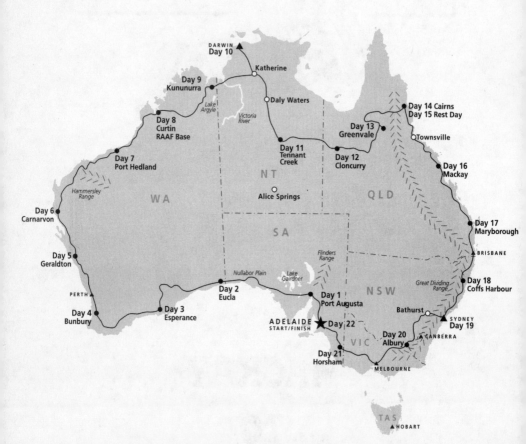

DARWIN
Day 10

Katherine

Day 9
Kununurra

Lake Argyle

Victoria River

Daly Waters

Day 8
Curtin
RAAF Base

Day 7
Port Hedland

Hammersley Range

Day 11
Tennant Creek

Day 13
Greenvale

Day 14 Cairns
Day 15 Rest Day

Townsville

Day 12
Cloncurry

Day 16
Mackay

N T

Alice Springs

W A

Day 6
Carnarvon

S A

Q L D

Day 17
Maryborough

Day 5
Geraldton

Flinders Range

BRISBANE

Nullabor Plain

Lake Gairdner

PERTH

Day 2
Eucla

Day 1
Port Augusta

N S W

Great Dividing Range

Day 18
Coffs Harbour

Day 4
Bunbury

Day 3
Esperance

Bathurst

Day 19

ADELAIDE
START/FINISH   **Day 22**

Day 20
Albury

SYDNEY

CANBERRA

V I C

Day 21
Horsham

MELBOURNE

T A S

HOBART

One of the challenges the PlayStation faced in its march down the coast was that, as it reached the more populated regions of Australia, it became progressively more difficult to locate potential competitive stages and then gain permission to include them. Many councils and, quite often, the Forestry Service, aren't always keen on having a rally run across their roads and tracks.

True to his word, Bob Carpenter had tried to find sections offering something for the rally cars, which were at their best on the smoother, faster roads, and also for the four-wheel drives, which, of course, really came good when the going got tough. This balancing act was extremely challenging, particularly on the east coast. After being able to find an array of tracks stretching for 100, often 200 km, in the outback, as the rally headed down the east coast this became almost impossible.

Never was this dilemma more obvious than on Day 17. Although the rally convoy would cover 825 km, there were just three competitive stages scheduled, totalling 92 km.

There wasn't too much in the way of competitive rallying on Day 17, but we were all determined to make the most of what we had. Because of the time Webby and I lost the day before, we were ninth away.

Stewart Lister, one of the course checkers, and a handy rally driver too, reckoned the first stage was the best stage of the entire event. And he had a point, for it was a brilliant piece of driver's road. However, given that it stretched to just less than 13 km, it was over almost before you had the chance to enjoy it.

The second stage, at 21 km, gave us a little more to get our teeth into, running along a well-surfaced shire road with lots of twists, turns and grids, not to mention a selection of crests so broad that not all of them were listed in the route instructions. In such circumstances a driver has to be able to 'read' the road. It was impossible and impractical for every trap to be cautioned. Consequently, rather than simply relying on instructions from the navigator, it was up to the driver to a large degree to rely on what he or she could see and feel.

Those who race over blind crests without being certain of what lies ahead, or lifting off without knowing where the road goes, are doomed to hit something sooner or later—the law of averages maintains that you won't get away with it all the time.

Unless I've seen, or can see, what's happening, or am told that the road *definitely* goes straight over a crest, I'll always play it safe. It is much better to sacrifice a couple of seconds rather than run the very real risk of ending up with a bent and broken vehicle. When it all boils down, a few seconds are worth nothing in an event that stretches over three weeks.

This is where the eyes of the co-driver are important as well. If there are no instructions to read, the navigator should also be looking ahead to try to see where the track goes. Two sets of eyes are definitely better than one.

The final run—based around the Broowena Forest, and the longest of the day at almost 58 km—was a real cracker. Running through both natural and pine-plantation forests, this stage had it all. Smooth and fast gravel, slippery clay, crests, twists, turns and a few wooden bridges which had as much grip as plastic covered with soap. In some places, it was also very rough, which was fine by us.

Despite my initial fears that the run down the coast would

leave our Jackaroo struggling against the far more agile rally cars, it wasn't working out that way. Indeed, I was constantly amazed that, on roads where I reckoned the cars would have beaten us hands down, we were more than holding our own and, quite often, beating them in a straight head-to-head contest.

Better yet, none of those chasing us had been able to chew into our time advantage although, similarly, Bruce was maintaining his upper hand in the lead. If we were going to win the PlayStation, it now looked like coming down to him making a mistake rather than us mounting a run from behind. However, judging by the way Bruce was pacing himself, that was a lot to hope for.

We enjoyed a good and uneventful run on the day, more than making up for our lack of direction on Day 16 and ending up second overall on the day. The only car in front of us for the day was the Wise/Long Commodore ute, which had been repaired after holing its sump and was back up and running, if not competing for outright honours.

The second Pedder's ute of company boss Ron Pedder and son Scott was going great guns, now running third overall after Reg Owen hit a bit of trouble in the big Nissan. And the Datsun was fourth, an amazing and heroic effort, having lost only two seconds on Day 17 in their epic battle with the Lockhart Jackaroo.

Maryborough showground put on a carnival atmosphere for the night's festivities, with amazing crowd numbers. Even Nigel Bolling's parents drove up from Noosa to see their son, probably to make sure he was doing his job. On that score, they needn't have worried, because Nigel had organised the servicing brilliantly, ensuring that both vehicles were in perfect shape each and every day and going to extraordinary lengths to make sure that the drivers' requests were carried out.

Nigel is no stranger to motorsport. He worked with Colin Bond for many years and knows exactly what it takes to keep a competitive car up and running. If we did make it home with a 1–2 result it would be a just and fitting reward for those who had put in the hard yards after the driving crew had finished theirs. Without their expertise the car I was driving wouldn't have reached Maryborough in anything like the position or condition it was in.

DAY 18

MARYBOROUGH
TO
COFFS HARBOUR

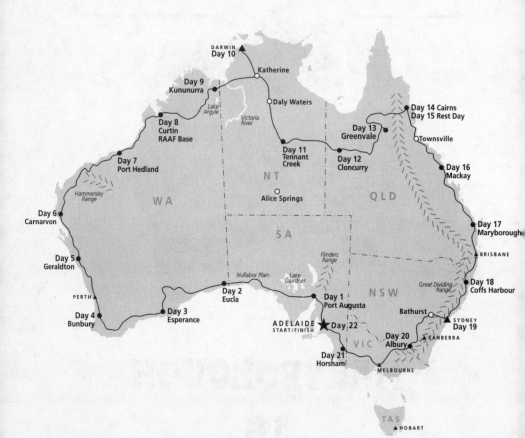

DARWIN
Day 10

Katherine

Daly Waters

Day 14 Cairns
Day 15 Rest Day

Day 9
Kununurra

Lake
Argyle

Victoria
River

Day 8
Curtin
RAAF Base

Day 11
Tennant
Creek

Day 13
Greenvale

Townsville

Day 7
Port Hedland

Day 12
Cloncurry

Day 16
Mackay

Hammersley
Range

N T

Alice Springs

W A

Q L D

Day 6
Carnarvon

S A

Day 17
Maryborough

Flinders
Range

Day 5
Geraldton

Nullabor Plain

Lake
Gairdner

BRISBANE

PERTH

Day 2
Eucla

Day 1
Port Augusta

N S W

Great Dividing
Range

Day 18
Coffs Harbour

Day 4
Bunbury

Day 3
Esperance

Bathurst

Day 19

SYDNEY

ADELAIDE
START/FINISH   **Day 22**

CANBERRA

Day 20
Albury

V I C

Day 21
Horsham

MELBOURNE

T A S

HOBART

The PlayStation was now in territory that should have suited the conventional rally cars much more than the four-wheel drives. These were roads where in normal circumstances a conventional rally car such as a Commodore should win back around three to four seconds per kilometre from vehicles such as the Jackaroos.

However, aware of criticisms of previous rallies that the east coast run might not have been challenging enough, PlayStation organisers were keen to keep the rally cars in check. But even with this philosophy in place, it was still a big effort for the leading Jackaroos to retain the bulk of the advantage they had built up in the outback of Western Australia.

When I'm at home on the farm back in Victoria, I usually get up early. I'm just not the type that can lay in bed or sit around doing nothing. Frankly it's not in my nature, I need to be up and doing things. For me, that's the key to getting the most from life and achieving things.

You can sit around and talk about things you'd like to do or actually get up off your butt and make things happen. That's the way I am, although I have to admit that even when I'm full of energy and keen to tackle a pet project, I'm not usually ready to get stuck into it at 4.00 am.

But that's what time we had to be away on Day 18. There were five short and sharp competitive stages on the agenda, all being run and won before we even reached Brisbane, which meant that after some frantic rally action during the first part of the day, we would then be condemned to a long transport down the coast. Such is the nature of a round-Australia event.

So the day held the promise of some fun in the forest. As a bonus, not everything about today's driving would suit the rally cars. I knew this because Bob Carpenter had told me he had decided to throw in something of a wild card.

He had scheduled just two service stops, one after the first 22 km special stage, and another at the end of the fifth and final effort of the day. This was to put some tactical thinking back into the way the day should be attacked, for if the rally cars went all out, they would quickly tear their tyres to shreds and be in big trouble as the day wore on. The trick would be to drive hard but with a degree of smoothness, to conserve the rubber. Obviously, the harder the tyre compound used, the better the wear rate, but that also meant that a driver would have to sacrifice grip for longevity.

Choosing the right tyres is something of an art form, be it in racing or rallying. Once upon a time, back when I started my career, you just leapt into a vehicle and drove it as hard as humanly possible, sometimes even harder, knowing that what you had was all there was available. However, in recent times, the myriad of new tyre compounds has dramatically increased the importance of good judgment by race team management. You have to balance grip and wear. A soft tyre will stick like glue and the car will corner brilliantly, meaning sensational lap times. But because it is soft it will wear rapidly and, eventually, lap times will fall away. Alternatively, a hard tyre will slip and slide early on and the car will be all over the place, but as the heat builds it will start to get stickier. A hard tyre will last much longer, but the sacrifice is that initial lack of grip.

No doubt everyone has heard in recent years the complaints of touring-car drivers as they put down their lack of performance, or the better performance of their rivals, to what rubber was mounted on the wheels. Bridgestone has, over the last few seasons, been the tyre to beat, and I enjoyed that advantage when I was leading the Mobil-Holden factory team.

By limiting service opportunities, Carpenter introduced an endurance way of thinking into a day that, for all intents and purposes, should have suited the sprint rally guys down to the ground. It was a clever and, as far as the four-wheel drive brigade was concerned, welcome move.

I was proud of the way our car was holding its own. Originally, I had expected to lose something like three or four seconds to the rally cars on stages such as these. The restrictions on service stops helped, but I felt that other factors played a part. One, we were very committed to showing the rally cars just how fair dinkum we were—so, for example, we didn't lose any speed at all through corners. And two, being taller, the Jackaroo's vision was so much better—this meant that we could see what was ahead, especially around corners, just that little, crucial bit better.

Because of all the rain that had fallen in the area, the roads were very slippery and, in places, quite rough, which helped offset the rally cars' balance of power. And anyway, forgetting our pursuers, I was still being constantly surprised at the abilities of the standard Jackaroo. Now that I *really* had a feel for the car, I was throwing it around with confidence. We slipped and slid around in what must have been spectacular style, but the big two-tonne 4 × 4 never let me down. It was always eager to please and amazingly responsive. In fact, it felt more like a nimble little rally car than a bulky four-wheel drive and even over the most narrow of forest trails, I could place it where I wanted to go.

Why had I waited so long to contest such an event in a big four-wheel drive? From now on, I don't think I ever want to attempt a rally like the PlayStation in a 'normal' car.

Of course, even with four-wheel drive, one should never underestimate the potential for disaster. Having all four wheels working in your favour is sensational, but it's not a miracle worker and if you do stray where angels fear to tread, well, you could be in big trouble.

Any car is only as good as the person at the wheel.

On the final stage of the day—a beaut 20 km run that started with a long, steep climb up a narrow trail, with some big drops on the side, and which then became a wide, open and very fast gravel road to the finish—Bruce Garland finally got it wrong.

After days of playing a game of safety first, Bruce had decided to have a bit of fun along this great slice of road. However, he somehow managed to spear off on a right-hand corner, flying over a fallen tree that was just off to the side of the road and plunging down a gully into a fence.

It could have been a disaster. The fence prevented him from going forward while the steepness of the bank, plus the fact that there was a tree laying across this escape route, made it impossible to go backwards either. In his frantic efforts to get out of there, he tried reversing as fast as he could ... but the Jackaroo just couldn't find the speed to climb and clear the fallen tree. All the while, time was ticking away.

He'd had more than a half an hour advantage at the beginning of the day and now here he was, stranded. Cruelly, his lead was all draining away. In endurance racing you can spend hours patiently edging away from your competition, but it takes just one mistake to wipe it all away. And that's what was happening to Bruce.

However, good fortune was on his side. The Mitsubishi Pajero of Warren and Joy Ridge, running seventh outright, blazed onto the scene, slid to a halt and grabbed Bruce's tow rope. With one mighty tug, the Jackaroo was freed from captivity. The total cost of the unplanned excursion was around six minutes. Bruce was still firmly in the lead, but we were now closer than we'd been for many days.

But close enough to mount a challenge? That was yet to be seen.

From the end of this stage nothing remained, aside from a 30-minute service stop in Kilcoy, until we reached our overnight destination of Coffs Harbour. To get to Coffs involved a 510 km run down the highway, broken only by a publicity stop at a shopping centre on the outskirts of Brisbane.

Faced with such a long highway run, I handed over the wheel duties to Webby and moved to the passenger side to brush up on my navigational skills. A few hours into the trip, having meandered down the highway and stopped occasionally for a little sightseeing as we passed through the coastal towns, I suddenly realised that we weren't going to make it to Coffs Harbour in the time allowed.

In fact we were going to be very late. To lose time on a transport stage is not something you want to do, so I encouraged Webby to press on. And that's what he did, sometimes flirting with the true spirit of the law, but equally determined that we wouldn't throw away any time by not reaching the control point at the Opal Cove Resort in Coffs Harbour at the appointed hour.

Webby was going as hard as he dared given that this was the main highway, but still things were looking grim. It was going to be tight as we rushed down the road past holiday spots such as Byron Bay, Ballina and into Grafton. Webby was still shaking his head when he grabbed the book off me, did his own mental calculations, and came to the conclusion that instead of being late, we'd actually be more than 90 minutes early.

It seems that my ability as a co-driver had been found somewhat lacking.

DAY 19

COFFS HARBOUR
TO
SYDNEY

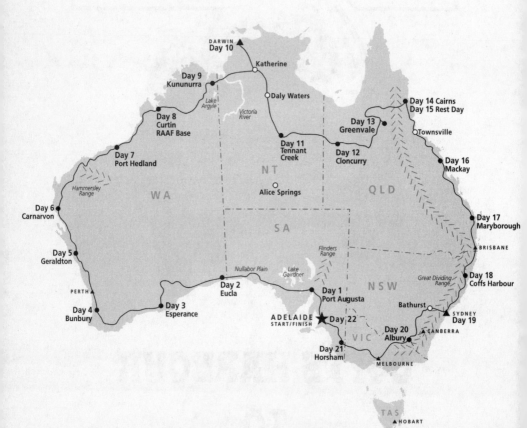

DARWIN
Day 10

Day 9
Kununurra

Katherine

Day 8
Curtin
RAAF Base

Lake
Argyle

Daly Waters

Victoria
River

Day 14 Cairns
Day 15 Rest Day

Day 7
Port Hedland

Day 11
Tennant
Creek

Day 13
Greenvale

Townsville

NT

Day 12
Cloncurry

Day 16
Mackay

Hammersley
Range

WA

Alice Springs

QLD

Day 6
Carnarvon

SA

Day 17
Maryborough

BRISBANE

Day 5
Geraldton

Flinders
Range

Day 18
Coffs Harbour

Nullabor Plain

Lake
Gairdner

Day 2
Eucla

Day 1
Port Augusta

Great Dividing
Range

NSW

PERTH

Bathurst

SYDNEY

Day 4
Bunbury

Day 3
Esperance

ADELAIDE
START/FINISH

Day 22

Day 19

CANBERRA

Day 20
Albury

VIC

Day 21
Horsham

MELBOURNE

TAS

HOBART

Back in the real heyday of Australian rallying, the 1970s, the premier event in the nation was, beyond any shadow of a doubt, the annual Southern Cross International. Not only was this the biggest rally in the nation—and remember this was well before staging a round of the World Championship in Australia was ever even considered—it was also our first truly international event.

Over the years it attracted the greatest stars of world rallying: legends of the sport such as Rauno Aaltonen, who was one of my team-mates in the 1979 Repco Trial, multiple winner and now Mitsubishi Ralliart boss, Andrew Cowan, and Ari Vatanen. It was also the happy hunting ground of local top guns such as Colin Bond, Greg Carr, George Fury, Ross Dunkerton and Barry Ferguson, and where the works teams from Ford, Nissan and Mitsubishi engaged in all-out dirt warfare once each year.

Barry, incidentally, was still plugging along in his 1976 VW Beetle in the 1998 PlayStation Rally.

It was in the forests and the mountains west of Coffs Harbour, Bellingen, Nambucca Heads, Macksville, Kempsey, Port Macquarie and Taree that these legends used to go into battle. Today, the PlayStation would use some of those stages.

These days, Western Australia may well be the home for the downunder round of the World Rally Championship but, as good as the roads around Perth may be, I have to say that it's on the New South Wales north coast that you'll find the finest rally terrain in the nation.

While many of the modern rally stages are little more than super-smooth dirt freeways, the route of the old Southern

Cross was a far more devious and testing affair. There were stages where speed and bravery meant everything, including a quick time, but on others, the rugged and sometimes brutal conditions meant that it was the ability to survive rather than how quick you went that mattered.

I had the time of my life. From the moment the first special stage of Day 19 began, we were left with little doubt that these stages would be some of the most demanding and taxing legs of our entire journey. As the rally guys like to say, Day 19 was all about rallying when 'cars had guts and men had balls'. This meant it was dangerous ... and a lot of fun.

Oh, and slippery too. Constant rain meant the stages offered all the grip of ice and it would have been a miracle if everyone had made it through unscathed. Of course, that didn't happen. For example on the fourth stage, which started out on a wide, smooth track but then entered a narrow valley that was basically nothing more than a greasy grass track, Keith Callinan (who was running 37th after his earlier problems) got his Commodore out of shape, went up a bank and rolled.

As we lined up for the start of the fifth and final stage of the day, Linda Long appeared at my window. Linda, co-driving for Graeme Wise in the Pedders Commodore ute, asked if it would be all right if they started ahead of us. We were running first on the road, having passed them on the previous stage.

We'd been able to sneak by on a superb 55 km section that had a little of everything—open plains, narrow forest tracks and cows, lots of cows. Indeed, it was probably the time Wise had lost threading his way through them that had allowed us to haul him in. But now they were worried that the final 52 km run of the day, which was to be held in some intimidating country, might be too much for the Commodore. If they went before us and struck trouble, they reasoned, we could help out.

In driving rain, we let them go first. A minute later, we set off in pursuit.

Their pessimism was well placed. Boy, what a nightmare this stage was. The rain was so heavy that it was practically impossible to see the road, which was so slippery even the Jackaroo had to fight hard to maintain its footing. We splashed and slithered along, then the call from Linda came over the radio ... their ute was bogged.

Soon after, we rolled through a creek crossing and found that they weren't just bogged, they were as good as buried in thick red clay. We stopped, let them connect a tow rope to our Jackaroo, and yanked them out. No problems!

I drove the stage as hard as I could, sliding and slipping and pushing the Jackaroo to the very limit. Finally, we reached the end of the stage, frankly overjoyed at the job we had done, only to be informed that the stage had been cancelled because of the weather. According to the control marshal, it was too wet and slippery for the non-four-wheel drives. After the early cars had set off, organisers had ruled that the constant downpour was turning things from extremely difficult to lethal and sent the rest of the field down the main highway.

Which was unfortunate, but their call. The Toyota 4 Runner of Tasmanians Steven and David Phillips and Jason Neasy had crashed into a bank before the stage was abandoned; perhaps this was a factor in the decision. All we could do was join the haul down to the Wyee truck stop, which is on the Newcastle-to-Sydney Freeway, before the run into the harbour city.

Big things had been planned for the arrival of the rally in Australia's biggest city, but things weren't going according to plan. The bad weather during the day had sent the timetable out the window. This, we learned later, caused a certain degree of panic among the entourage in Sydney. We were asked to make haste and cut our service time at Wyee down to a bare minimum, ensuring only that our crew had a good chance to give the Jackaroo a once-over, before making the dash down the highway.

Even in the driving rain, the first look at the Sydney skyline was spectacular. I don't care how much people rave about going overseas, this is surely one of the great cities of the world. As we drove across the Harbour Bridge and looked across to the Opera House, even this parochial Melbourne boy had to admit that Sydney was indeed a glorious place. Sure, it may lack the sophisticated lifestyle and weather we enjoy down south, but you can't say it's not pretty.

Despite the rain and our late entrance there was a good crowd waiting for us as we rolled into Darling Harbour, although with a couple of sponsors' functions to attend we didn't get to our hotel opposite the Sydney Entertainment Centre until late at night.

Looking after the sponsors is a necessary part of any professional sport and probably even more so in motor racing. A tennis player needs a pair of shorts, shoes, a shirt and a racket to participate. A golf player a respectable set of duds and a set of clubs. But to go motor racing we're talking big dollars. You need a car, a gifted crew, tyres and talent as well. Money can't buy talent, but it can get all the other ingredients, so it pays to give something back to the backers, for without them you could easily be out of a job.

Unfortunately, far too many drivers reckon that sponsorship is a God-given right, but it is anything but. No one is bigger than the sport, which is why I always try to do the right thing by my sponsors. In this case, had it not been for the backing of AMP I wouldn't even have been in the PlayStation Rally.

Indeed, without PlayStation there may not have been a rally to worry about in the first place.

It was interesting to sit back for a moment and compare the people at the Sydney function to those who had attended the outback gatherings along the route. No surprises really, it was the relative sophistication of the crowd that stood out. It is really quite extraordinary how we think we are the same all over the country, when really we are quite diverse. At Darling Harbour, it appeared that most of the gentlemen had come straight from the board room—best gear on, hair slicked back, looking good. The women were beautifully dressed. In the bush the guys are a little more blasé than the fellas from the cities, so it was more 'smart casual'. A smattering of RM Williams, a few ties, the odd jacket. And the further you got away from the big cities, the more casual the women dressed, though they were always well presented.

But to a certain extent off-road endurance rallies aren't big city stuff. Rallies are more about 'Australiana' than what the slickers from the CBD call 'motorsport'. Their preference is generally the glitz and glamour of the Grand Prix and the touring cars.

DAY 20

SYDNEY
TO
ALBURY

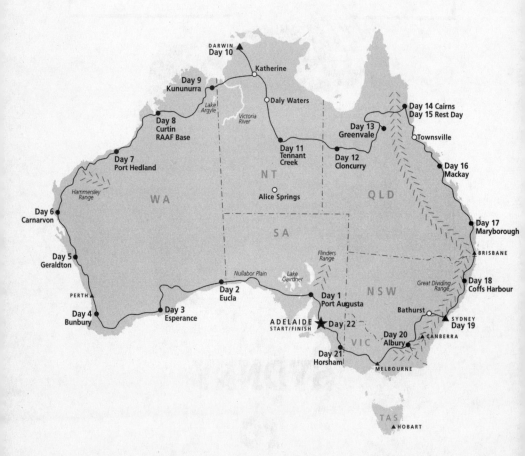

DARWIN
Day 10

Katherine

Daly Waters

Day 9
Kununurra

Lake
Argyle

Victoria
River

Day 8
Curtin
RAAF Base

Day 14 Cairns
Day 15 Rest Day

Townsville

Day 13
Greenvale

Day 11
Tennant
Creek

Day 12
Cloncurry

Day 16
Mackay

Day 7
Port Hedland

Hammersley
Range

N T

Alice Springs

W A

Q L D

Day 6
Carnarvon

S A

Day 17
Maryborough

Day 5
Geraldton

Flinders
Range

BRISBANE

Nullabor Plain

Lake
Gairdner

Day 2
Eucla

Day 1
Port Augusta

N S W

Great Dividing
Range

Day 18
Coffs Harbour

PERTH

Bathurst

Day 4
Bunbury

Day 3
Esperance

Day 19
SYDNEY

CANBERRA

ADELAIDE
START/FINISH **Day 22**

Day 20
Albury

V I C

Day 21
Horsham

MELBOURNE

T A S

HOBART

Organisers had Sydney's inevitably congested traffic in mind when they ruled that for this one day, they would do away with the typical starting procedure where vehicles leave at one minute intervals. To avoid the peak hour rush (which is actually a misnomer given that in most large cities this 'rush' now takes upwards of three hours to complete) the field departed from Darling Harbour, en masse, at 5.00 am.

Meanwhile, Rob Gambino and David Lowe had now set their sights on the third-placed Nissan Patrol of Reg Owen and Russell Cairns, after appearing to finally shake off the persistent Lockhart/Donovan Jackaroo. The Datsun was now 40 minutes clear of the Jackaroo, which had suffered numerous problems during the second stage outside of Coffs Harbour. Another car to struggle was the Commodore driven by Peter Champion and Ken Long, who were impeded by a broken diff.

Only a little more than five minutes separated the third and fourth cars. 'They'll catch us,' predicted Owen, when asked about the 'harassment' he'd been copping from the rampaging 180B.

That prophecy was going to come true quicker than he anticipated.

The combination of our late arrival and the foul weather on the previous night meant only a relatively small gathering of grimly enthusiastic spectators had been able to get a look at the field. Now, our departure in the early morning darkness deprived fans of a second opportunity to catch up with the PlayStation competitors. Which was a great shame. However, if leaving early meant an easier escape from the city, I was all for it.

Our first port of call for the day was to be Lithgow, a historical coal-mining town. Here the field, scrambled because of the shotgun start, would be regrouped into the appropriate running order based on the finishing positions of the previous day.

Therefore, we would be the first car away, our times from the previous day giving us a head start over Graeme Wise in the Commodore ute, and Bruce Garland. Bruce, however, maintained his commanding lead, while we remained in second place, well ahead of Reg Owen's Nissan. Barring a major mistake on our part, we didn't really have to worry about Reg catching us, but he was coming under huge pressure from the dynamic Datsun duo of Gambino and Lowe.

Our route, west out of Sydney, took us up through the apple-growing area around Bilpin, along Bell's Line of Road. Most motoring enthusiasts will know this section of bitumen for it's one of the great driving roads, although it can be busy and the police are aware just how much fun it is to have a speed along here.

It was freezing when we arrived in Lithgow. It was quite a sight to see crews and competitors rummaging through their vehicles to break out jumpers and rally jackets, items of clothing most hadn't laid eyes on since our departure from Adelaide almost three weeks ago. To think, just a week or so ago we were racing in 40 degrees Celsius plus temperatures and now, here we were, shivering in frigid conditions.

But it wasn't the cold that was the real problem, it was the rain that was causing some major headaches. It had been bucketing down in this area for days. Given that the normal conditions—dry—of this opening stage are atrocious, the organisers now reckoned that given its saturated state, it would prove to be impassable. And we learned that stage three was gone as well, because tree logging had blocked the way through. It was decided that some rapid and hectic changes would be made to the route, but unfortunately, some of the revised instructions were either confusing or wrong. This led to a large proportion of the field racing up and down the highway searching for a right turn that allegedly led to the start of the first stage.

Finally, after some animated chat over the two-ways, we arrived at the opening stage of the day, ironically well before it was ready to be opened for competition. Before unleashing cars on any stage, an official vehicle has to drive along the route first to ensure that it is safe—that there is no 'civilian' traffic on the course and that access from sidetracks has been blocked off. Because of the last-minute changes this process hadn't been completed, which left us with time to kill ...

So we did what anyone does when out in the bush. We built a fire—as much for the atmosphere as to keep warm—and stood around telling each other lies about what we'd been up to in the event so far. Pretty soon the entire field was standing around having a chat, which gave us the chance to get a group photo of the PlayStation class of '98.

Nothing beats a little local knowledge, and Linda Long had managed to pick up some inside information from a friend who lived in the area. Thankfully she shared it with Webby, so we now knew which corners were especially slippery, where the track was really boggy and the locations of some very rough patches where caution would be the order of the day.

This intelligence proved very, very helpful, because the 48 km stage, called 'Dark Corner', was a real mixture, some of the roads being fast and wide while elsewhere the track was narrow and offered almost nothing in the way of grip. Not only did we make it through the stage unscathed, we were actually the fastest. There was also one section that took us along a rough and rocky fire trail, which featured a steep descent leading into a T-junction where it would have been oh so easy to overshoot.

As far as I was concerned, the opening stage was just a warm-up for the one I was really looking forward to. This was a stage scheduled on Mt Panorama at Bathurst. Initially, I had hoped that we'd get to blaze around the circuit itself, for I didn't think I'd need any navigational input to help me find my way around that 6.17 km of bitumen.

However, that wasn't to be the case. Instead, we would be using a combination of the access road to the top of the mountain and then part of the camping areas, Reid and McPhillamy parks.

I've been to Bathurst on many, many occasions, but I can't claim to have a deep knowledge of this part of the circuit. It was certainly a different slice of Mt Panorama to what I'd been used to for 30-odd years and I just hoped that I didn't get lost. It would have been pretty embarrassing.

Before we headed to the track there was a quick service and publicity stop in the car park of the Bathurst McDonald's. The crowd roll up was amazing.

Given my close relationship with the city, you could say that Bathurst is like my second home. When we pulled into the parking area, I was a bit overwhelmed at the size of the crowd that had turned up to say hello and wish us luck. And there were some real diehard Brock fans among them, including one guy who had my autograph tattooed on his chest. Seriously! A couple of years before, I had scrawled by signature on his chest with a black marker pen and he'd immediately raced down to the local tattoo parlour and had it etched in permanently. Now that's a fan.

Others had put together incredibly intricate and elaborate banners of encouragement. I was overwhelmed. Sometimes during this adventure, I had to admit that the level of fanaticism of some fans stopped me in my tracks. Some people go to extraordinary lengths to show their support.

And don't for a minute think that I don't appreciate their backing. When so many people put in so much time it's only right to try to offer as much time as possible—to have a chat, sign a few autographs and pose for some photographs. Supporting me means so much to some people, and me returning their support means so much to me, that I simply find it impossible to say no. This meant that sometimes during the PlayStation Webby had to drag me away from a crowd and force me back into the Jackaroo or else we would have missed our starting position.

It was like this at Bathurst. There was another large crowd waiting at the top of Mt Panorama to say G'day and see the action. Before we began there was a little matter of voting in the upcoming federal election. A special 'Checkpoint Charlie' had been set up on the mountain for competitors and fans to lodge absentee votes during the AMP Bathurst 1000 weekend a week later, and I was only too happy to cast my vote early and promote the existence of the polling booth.

Quite a tricky little stage this Mt Panaroma section was, too. Just four kilometres long, but it zigged and zagged around the camping area at such a pace that Webby was struggling to read me the instructions in time for me to make all the turns. It wasn't a perfect stage for the Jackaroo, but I was happy to find that we managed the fourth-fastest time overall and were the quickest of the four-wheel drives.

Of course, I had hoped that somehow we could have won that stage. Maybe, I'd joked to reporters, such a result would have been the 10th victory at Bathurst which everyone had wanted so badly.

After Bathurst we faced a long transport stage. We drove through Cowra, along the Olympic Way, then went through Harden, and made a fuel stop at that genuine Aussie icon— the Dog on the Tuckerbox, which I'm sure everyone knows is five miles from Gundagai. From there, we headed out towards Tumut and then along the Snowy Mountains Highway for the last competitive outing of the day.

The final sprint of the day was a 56 km dash that started on a well-maintained and fast tourist road, but evolved into narrow tracks as we climbed further into the mountains. There was some pretty challenging stuff. In places there were stretches of slippery red clay that was a real trap for the unwary and those who didn't have their mind completely on the job.

The final service of the day was in the lovely little village of Tumbarumba. Around 1600 people live in this sheltered little hamlet, although tourists swell that number considerably during the ski season. I reckon that most of them were waiting to greet us when we rolled into the local showground for a 10-minute stop. Certainly, I had no chance of working my way through all the autograph hunters before it was time to head off for our overnight stop in Albury, a further 150 km down the road.

Depending on whom you listen to, Albury is famous as the home of country music superstar Lee Kernaghan or race driver Brad Jones. I reckon that just about everyone has heard of Lee Kernaghan, but Brad Jones?

Brad was once my team-mate, back in the days when I ran

a couple of Ford Sierras in the Australian Touring Car Championship. A fine driver, and successful too, having collected a fistful of national Auscar championships, Nascar titles and, in an Audi, a pair of two-litre Super Touring National Championships. He's also a regular in the V8 battles at Bathurst.

Brad has his workshop in Albury and normally we would have caught up when I rolled into town. However, he'd departed for Bathurst to prepare for the AMP 1000 the following week. So instead, it was a quiet night at the hotel. The next day would be the final full day of competition, before we headed into Adelaide for the finish.

It was a pretty relaxed night for our crew for the Jackaroo was in near-perfect shape and running like a train. This may sound like an advertisement, but the Jackaroo had really amazed me during the event. Considering it was basically a stock-standard machine, it performed brilliantly, for while it was giving away a considerable amount of power to some of our modified rivals, it had regularly beaten nearly all of them in competitive stages.

This had been true again on Day 20; we would lead the field away from Albury in the morning. However, in the battle for outright honours, Bruce Garland still had his hands wrapped around the victory trophy.

The big story of the day in terms of the race standings was that the relentless pursuit by the Datsun boys, Rob Gambino and David Lowe, had finally produced a result. With Reg Owen striking a problem in his Nissan, rolling it on the first stage of the day to drop the Patrol back to sixth outright, the 180B had leapt into a podium position.

'It was our first mistake,' rued Russell Cairns afterwards. All up, they'd lost 22 minutes waiting for help to get the big, heavy Nissan back on four wheels. 'Still,' he continued, 'the Datsun would have caught us anyway, so it's only going to cost us one place.'

It just shows what can be achieved if you never give up and stay focused. Sure, they'd had their setbacks during the course of the event, but in situations where many others might have thrown their hands in the air and lost the plot, these two kept their heads down and battled on regardless. Now they were third outright, in a car which had all but chalked up a quarter of a century of work. Amazing!

Reg Owen's accident had also allowed the Jackaroo of Peter Lockhart to jump up into fourth place, while Warren Ridge now had his Mitsubishi Pajero in fifth.

Everyone, from first to last, remained mindful that there was still a day-and-a-half of competition in store for the PlayStation field. And everyone involved in motorsport knows only too well that the counting of chickens before any eggs have hatched is fraught with danger and a certain recipe for disappointment.

There was still much rallying to do before anyone could savour the taste of the finish-line champagne.

On Day 21, we were to find out just how true these clichés are . . .

DAY 21

ALBURY

TO

HORSHAM

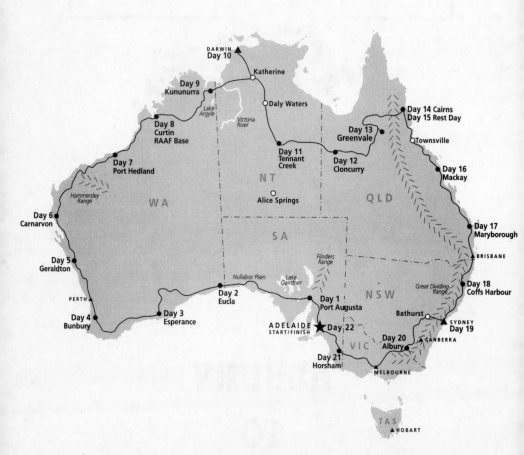

DARWIN
Day 10 ▲

Katherine

Daly Waters ○

Day 9
Kununurra ●

*Lake
Argyle*

Day 8
**Curtin
RAAF Base** ●

*Victoria
River*

Day 13
Greenvale ●

Day 14 Cairns
Day 15 Rest Day ●

Townsville ○

Day 7
Port Hedland ●

*Hammersley
Range*

Day 11
**Tennant
Creek** ●

Day 12
Cloncurry ●

Day 16
Mackay ●

N T

Alice Springs ○

Q L D

W A

Day 6
Carnarvon ●

S A

Day 17
Maryborough ●

Day 5
Geraldton ●

*Flinders
Range*

▲ BRISBANE

Nullabor Plain

*Lake
Gairdner*

Day 2
Eucla ●

Day 1
Port Augusta ●

N S W

*Great Dividing
Range*

Day 18
Coffs Harbour ●

PERTH ○

Bathurst ○

Day 4
Bunbury ●

Day 3
Esperance ●

▲ SYDNEY
Day 19

ADELAIDE
START/FINISH ★ **Day 22**

Day 20
Albury ●

▲ CANBERRA

V I C

Day 21
Horsham ●

MELBOURNE ▲

T A S

▲ HOBART

One of the highlights of the PlayStation for two motor racing enthusiasts from Ararat in country Victoria, Ted Rogers and Alan Cameron, was the chance to drive their GTR Torana XU1 on home soil during the penultimate day of the event. This day was to take the field from the major Victoria–New South Wales border crossing at Albury to Horsham in western Victoria, and featured a special stage in the Mount Cole forest near Warrak, which is not too far off the Ararat to Horsham highway.

The Torana would eventually finish third overall in the historic car section of the race, first in the under-3.5 litre section and 16th outright.

For all the competitors, whether they were familiar with the territory or not, it was imperative that they keep their concentration. Disaster might only be one lapse in judgment away, as Peter Lockhart in his Jackaroo was about to discover. Even Peter Brock needed to be careful . . .

I've been in situations where the chequered flag has been in sight, only to have the car fail and grind to a halt. It's happened to everyone in racing. No sooner are you practising your victory speech . . . something catastrophic will happen.

Webby was telling me that the time had come, once and for all, to accept that we had second place nailed down and we could just cruise to the finish and collect the accolades for a good effort. We'd shadowed team leader Garland for the best part of two weeks. When Bruce moved into the lead on Day Six, we moved into second. Nothing had changed since then and it was highly unlikely anything would change between now and the end. The time had come, reasoned Webby, to take it easy, back off the gas and enjoy the ride to the end.

After all, it really was just about over bar the shouting. Only five relatively short stages on this day, another two tomorrow and then we'd be at the finish in Adelaide. It would all be over. I wasn't feeling disappointed, for I'd enjoyed a marvellous three weeks, both in competition and through meeting so many people around the nation. But in the back of my mind, I couldn't help thinking how nice it would be to win.

We'd pushed hard since Day One, but it was almost certain that we would run second to Bruce. This was a brilliant result for the team. Bruce had earned it, driving superbly and smartly for the entire event, pushing hard when he had to and taking it easy when it was needed. He'd put together the whole superb effort and he would deserve all the recognition he was going to get.

However, despite all this, I just couldn't bring myself to take it easy. There's something about being in a competitive vehicle on a competitive stage that makes it impossible to not try hard, and even though we had nothing to gain in terms of outright position, there was a degree of personal satisfaction to consider. So I kept pushing hard ... and enjoying myself.

And anyway, a professional racing driver *never* gives up, under any circumstances. Every time you get behind the wheel in a race you drive fast, because that is what you are all about.

Continuing this approach wasn't hard, for the opening two stages of the day in Victoria's breathtaking high country captured what rallying is all about. This was rally country at its best. In the second stage, which featured plenty of crests and turns as we ran along a high ridge line, we also encountered plenty of drop-offs where, according to the notes, you'd be able to celebrate a couple of birthdays before hitting the bottom. My navigator reckoned the drops were always on his side, but I did take time to point out that if he did fall off the edge, because I was in the car with him, I'd go as well. And I had no intention of falling off the side of the world just to spoil his day.

It was, to be honest, a little intimidating in places. There were plenty of opportunities to have an accident, which unfortunately is just what happened to Peter Lockhart, running fourth outright until he careered off the road and somehow managed to get his Jackaroo wedged in a culvert.

By the time they managed to extract him, and indeed that took a considerable amount of effort and ingenuity, he had dropped to 34th place and, with a broken rear drivetrain, faced the prospect of limping to the finish in the only known front-wheel drive Jackaroo in the world. Yet again, here was a good indication of just how quickly the tables can turn in motorsport.

The third stage of the day was named 'Mount Disappointment'. Sadly, for the 05 Jackaroo, what an apt name it turned out to be. This was a spectacular forest stage—fast, smooth and flowing, with quite a few spectactors to be seen in the bush. Midway through the stage, we entered a fast right-hand bend and the Jackaroo slid across the road, scrambling for grip, before it hit a gutter and turned onto its side. From here we slid along an embankment before striking a grassy mound. That impact actually pushed the car back onto its wheels. It was all so fast, I almost didn't have time to work out what was happening.

The episode was over in a matter of seconds; I reckon we lost next to no time at all. From inside, it appeared that the only casualties had been the rear passenger-side window, which had exploded on impact, and the rear passenger door—the one that gave us access to the fuel filler on our race-approved petrol tank—which had taken a thrashing and would require some work to get it open again.

Certainly, there appeared to be nothing that the guys couldn't handle at the next service stop at Somerton, just on the outskirts of Melbourne. However, it encourage Webby to once again stress the 'cruise and collect' theory that had now become his mantra.

There were only two stages left in the day, both relatively short forest runs, and then we could think about the finish. But first we had a publicity stop at a Westfield Shoppingtown on the outskirts of Melbourne, where I did my usual autograph session and chatted with the crowd. Then we headed towards Ballarat and the second-last competitive stage of the day.

This went without a hitch, leaving just one more to complete a long day on the road . . .

Only a few hundred metres and one bend into the last stage of the day, a little 16 km run in the Mount Cole forest, I pitched the Jackaroo into an innocuous-looking left-hander, one which angled slightly downhill. From the outset, it appeared to be no more difficult than any of the thousands of other corners we'd encountered so far during the epic.

But this one *was* different. The sandy covering over the hard road base made it as slippery as a newly-waxed kitchen floor. As we began to swerve, the rear of the Jackaroo broke loose and started sliding towards the edge of the road, which ended rather dramatically with a drop into a cleared gully a couple of metres lower than the main track.

I almost caught the pirouette before it got out of control. I had wound on full opposite lock and reckoned that, at worst, we'd escape with a minor spin. But then the rear wheel popped over the edge of the road and into clear air. The back of the

Jackaroo went down and the front went up and over she went. We rolled. She went over once completely before coming to rest on the passenger side. No sooner had we come to this brutal halt than Webby was on the radio, warning the rest of the field at the starting line of our situation. He clearly didn't relish the thought of the next vehicle through doing the same thing and ending up on top of us.

Webby was okay, though practically buried under the combination of junk that had been hanging around the cockpit—old sandwiches, empty drink bottles and his collection of road books and instructions. I struggled out of my harness and clambered out to survey the damage, fearing the worst. Was there any way the Jackaroo, as tough as it had proved to be, could escape from this without some major damage? To have come so far only to falter, almost in sight of the finish, was going to be tough. The big fear was that the engine had over-revved as we rolled or that one of the wheels had been torn off.

No sooner had I jumped down from the Jackaroo than help was on the scene. Ross Nicastri, now strictly an observer and standing a few hundred metres further down the road, had seen the crash and grabbed a few other spectators; they were already trying to lift the vehicle back onto its wheels. We all started to push and pull, trying to rock a couple of tonnes of Jackaroo back upright, but there just weren't enough of us.

Then Bruce Garland's Jackaroo slid to a halt on the road above us. One look, and he took a snap decision to tow us back onto the wheels. Webby had foraged in the back of our vehicle for the tow rope, which we attached to the hook on the front and then hitched to Bruce's Jackaroo. It was about now that Bruce came up with a brilliant idea. Instead of merely pulling our Jackaroo upright, he reckoned that with a big enough tug he could actually drag it back onto the road. And so he dropped the clutch and went spearing down the road.

The chain of events that followed was straight out of a TV comedy. The giant pull did indeed drag the Jackaroo upright, but it also ripped our tow hook straight out of the chassis and it went slicing through the air, slamming into Bruce's door and ripping out a big chunk of metal. Had anyone been standing in the hook's path they would be dead, but later on Bruce was dirtier about the fact that he now had a big hole in the side of his vehicle. When the tow hook parted company with our vehicle, there was nothing holding it at all—with ever-increasing momentum, it started rolling over and over, beating itself to bits before it finally came to a halt ... back on all fours but not looking particularly good.

I ended up standing behind it, which was not the place to be, for as everyone started to scream at me to get out of the way, it started to roll backwards towards me. After the original roll I had left it out of gear and without the handbrake on, and now it was threatening to run me over. I was backpedalling like a man possessed, but it was gaining on me. It was winning the race when my legs caught a tree stump and over I went, landing on my back. Fortunately, the Jackaroo brought itself to a stop, well away from where I ended up.

But there was no time to even think about what could have happened. Webby was already gathering up his instructions and the other gear that had been spread over the countryside, while I leapt back into the driver's seat and, with my heart in my mouth, tried the ignition. The engine fired up immediately, and sounded as healthy as it had ever had.

The next step was to see if it actually would drive, which

amazingly it did. So, cautiously, very cautiously, we tiptoed along the clearing until we found a way back onto the road and then gingerly headed towards the end of the stage. All the while, dust was cascading in through the broken windows and the rear door, which was jammed open, while Bruce rode shotgun to make sure we made it home.

I've never been so happy to see the end of a stage. Once we'd completed the paperwork, we drove a little further down the road before stopping to survey the damage. And there was plenty to survey.

Not one panel had escaped unscathed, a couple of windows were broken, one of the headlights was hanging out, held only by the wiring, and the satellite phone aerial was completely destroyed. Yet as we walked around the battered Jackaroo I started to feel increasingly cheerful. It appeared that the only real concern was how to tape the rear door closed to prevent us choking on the dust that came in. As for the drivers— Webby and I looked like the WWII panzer commanders you see in those old movies, the only white bits of skin being where our sunglasses had sat. The rest was all dusty brown, but a good shower would take care of that.

Webby reckoned he had a sore shoulder, but I think he was either after the sympathy vote or planned to sue for worker's compensation. He would get neither from me, for already I was trying to think of a way to blame it on him. One thing was certain, however. When we checked into service at the end of the day's racing, the Jackaroo crew would have a major panel beating job on its hands.

Now a lot of crews would complain and whinge if, on the home stretch, a driver had damaged the car by pushing unnecessarily, but that wasn't the case here. Instead, these guys relished the task of righting our wrong. They threw themselves into the job of getting the Jackaroo back into an acceptable state, aided by the kind generosity of other competitors who offered their equipment and, in the case of Warren Ridge, panel beating expertise to get us shipshape again. Ridge had his own vehicle to worry about, and he was running fourth at this stage, but he still gave his time to help our crew. I keep saying it over and over again—it's that kind of spirit that makes events like the PlayStation so special.

After much effort, including the use of some heavy-duty equipment to straighten the panels, the Jackaroo looked respectable. Maybe not as it did when it left the factory, for the driver's-side window was now perspex and the windscreen was held in by race tape, but from a distance it didn't look all that bad. It's just when you got up close that you could see first-hand what a mess we'd made.

Funnily enough, only a few days before, Webby had commented that the Jackaroo was in such pristine condition that it certainly didn't look like it had competed in a round-Australia rally. He reckoned that it needed a few more dings and dents to give it an authentic look. Well, at least now it looked like a veteran!

We'd make it to the finish if I had to carry the bloody thing.

DAY 22

HORSHAM
TO
ADELAIDE (THE END!)

The Datsun 180B of Gambino and Lowe had become the 'cult hero' of the PlayStation. They had driven an extremely clever race, being conservative early before attacking once the race reached the east coast. In the end they would finish third, a bit more than two-and-a-half hours behind the Jackaroo driven by Garland/Suzuki and a fraction over two hours behind the Brock/Webster Jackaroo.

'Our main problem was with tyres,' Gambino would tell *The Advertiser's* Bob Jennings when they finally returned to Adelaide. 'We thought we would get through on 12, but halfway up the west coast we were running out.

'By Darwin we were desperate. We got four more tyres [to get us] to Cloncurry and the eight we were supposed to get at Cairns didn't reach us until we were in Maryborough.

'At that point we were trying to catch the four-wheel drives and the only way we could do that was by throwing fresh tyres on the car.'

On the other hand, Ballarat's Russell McKenzie, who with co-driver Murray Rogers finished 13th in their 1983 VH Commodore, reckoned he got through the event without blowing one tyre.

'Sure, we bent a few rims, but we did not puncture one tyre,' he told a journalist from his hometown paper, the *Courier*. 'The roads were very unkind, with a lot of them suited only to the four-wheel drives. But by using your nous before attacking you could get through.'

McKenzie immediately said that he would like to go around the event course again, only this time with his family and with enough time to take in some scenery.

'If you asked me where we've been,' he admitted, 'I wouldn't really know.'

It's amazing how the mind works isn't it? As we left Adelaide three weeks ago for an incredible odyssey and one hell of an adventure, most of us were already thinking about the finish.

Now, as we stood on the doorstep of the finish, it seemed hard to imagine that it was all about to end. Over the course of three weeks, through the good times and the bad, we'd worked ourselves into something of a routine. It seemed natural to get up early, drive all day along some of the toughest roads imaginable, fix the vehicles at night and then grab a little much-needed sleep so that we could do it all again the next day.

But after today that routine would stop. Tomorrow, everyone would start to head home to pick up the pieces of their 'normal' existence. Even though I was looking forward to getting back to the farm to spend some time with Bev and the kids, it did feel strange.

Not that we were going to get off lightly just because it was the last day of school. No sir, that's not the way the PlayStation Rally was run.

The first vehicle would leave Horsham at 5.00 am, so there was no sleeping in to mark graduation day.

Instead of just shooting down the highway, Bob Carpenter had found a more scenic route for the first stage of the day and the second-last of the rally. He wanted to end with something a little more interesting than just a tour down a straight section of blacktop, and frankly that suited me just fine.

Unfortunately though, it was hard to appreciate the scenery given that a thick blanket of fog made it difficult to see anything much further than the end of the bonnet of the Jackaroo. It was real pea-soup stuff. The route Bob had chosen took us straight past Mount Arapiles and, thankfully, the fog lifted just in time for us to see this most amazing and incredible rock formation. The way it loomed out of the mist was breathtaking. It was filed away in the Brock memory bank as a place I would return to visit again one day when there was more time available to have a good look around.

We had a 160 km run to the first stage, which had been given the challenging title of 'Who Dares Wins'. We may have been heading for the finish, but once into the competitive side of things for the day, it quickly became obvious that Bob Carpenter wasn't about to make life any easier just because we were having our last day at the office.

The field had to tackle a phenomenal 69 km blast across western Victoria's Big Desert, along a track across dozens of sandy crests that would launch the cars in spectacular fashion. Because of our dramas on the previous day we started in 14th place, meaning that, given the nature of this terrain, we would have to catch and pass some of the slower vehicles that had jumped in front of us before the end of the leg. With some incredibly long straights, the Jackaroo was often at full pace for a considerable length of time, reeling in the vehicles in front.

But there was a need for caution, as the sandy track held plenty of traps: tight bends appearing almost out of nowhere, making us struggle for traction. There were a few spots, after some particularly big jumps, where the surroundings indicated that not all the cars in front of us had been in complete control as they dealt with the conditions. A couple of road signs had been knocked over, demonstrating that some drivers were still pushing their vehicles to the limit.

It was truly a brilliant stage, one that would capture the imagination of any driver, and we didn't have a problem—a tribute to the Garland crew and their specially conscripted cohorts who'd patched the car up so effectively after the carnage of yesterday. With the stage over, we were left with only a relatively short transport leg to a brief service stop in Pinnaroo—a town which sits on the Ouyen Highway just on the South Australian side of the border—before it was time for the last roll of the dice.

The last stage summed it all up. It was called 'Now or Never'.

This was a 22 km gravel stage over some superb, undulating country roads, complete with a couple of causeways that were cautioned and tricky. Certainly, it paid to be watchful, for to come this far and crash on the last stage would have been a total disaster.

Webby made it clear that I should do nothing more than drive around in first gear. But after three weeks sharing the cockpit with me, I reckoned he should have known better.

A large number of spectators had turned out for this final blast of the PlayStation Rally Round Australia 1998 and I, for one, reckon that when people take the time and trouble to head out to an event like this they deserve to be entertained. So, final stage or not, I went for it. On one corner I had the back hanging out so far that I clipped a plastic roadside marker. But I wasn't being reckless, just responding to what the punters wanted.

Fans don't want to see second best. This is what modern-day, professional sport is all about. In many ways, it's what life is all about too.

And then it was all over bar the shouting. All that remained was the haul down the highway into Adelaide for a regroup at the Victoria Park Racecourse on the edge of town before we headed in reverse order to the finish line in Rundle Street, where it had all started 22 days before.

I asked Webby how he felt now that it was all over and, for the first time in the 20-odd years that we've known each other, he struggled for the right words.

'I think, Brock,' he finally began with a sincerity that caught me by surprise, 'that it's absolutely brilliant that Bruce has won this event. This is Bruce's life, it's what he lives for, and I reckon it's fantastic that he's won the bloody thing.'

And he meant it.

We left Victoria Park second to last, only Garland and Suzuki being left to follow as the winners of the event. Among those not far in front of us was the Commodore ute of Ron and Scott Pedder, who had grabbed sixth place outright after a mighty effort to overtake the Falcon XR6 of Kevin Edwards and Martin Reeves on the final two stages of the day. Talk about leaving it to the last moment. Fifth was the Nissan Patrol of Reg Owen and Russell Cairns, with the always smiling Warren Ridge and wife Joy in their Mitsubishi Pajero (fourth) and that amazingly ancient Datsun 180B of never-say-die duo Robert Gambino and David Lowe (third) between Reg and us.

At the presentation dinner that night Lowe would give one of the longest acceptance speeches in the history of rallying— one that would have sparked a commercial break during the Academy Awards or a hook from stage left in Vaudeville. There was neither a commercial to throw to nor a hook to be found in the Adelaide Convention Centre, but these guys deserved a moment of glory for they had truly done an astounding job.

Heaven forbid if they ever turn up together in something built this century for a round-Australia event.

The crowd that had gathered in Rundle Street was colossal. People lined the footpaths on both sides and crowded around the Jackaroo, while radio and TV crews battled to get close enough to grab a few words on the event.

It was a sensational welcome back. Other crews who had already crossed the finish line were standing outside the bars, the start of long hauls towards hangovers; it was clear that the party had started without us. Finally, we crossed the line and did the mandatory leap onto the roof of the Jackaroo, not that it could cause any more damage to that already inflicted by the rollover the previous day.

And then it was time to move forward to allow Bruce and Harry to bask in the glory and accept the accolades that were rightfully theirs.

Eventually, we parked side-by-side, as the team celebrated its 1–2 finish. As Webby had said, it was very satisfying to see Bruce get the recognition he deserved. He had made the effort and meticulously built the vehicles. I can't think of anyone I would have rather seen spraying the victory champagne.

Understandably, both he and Harry were over the moon. Unless you've ever been involved in an event like this, you really can't understand just how hard it is to finish, let alone win. All four of us sat on the roof of my Jackaroo, after Bruce decided that he didn't want to damage his relatively intact machine. The 05 car was, as he gently put it, 'rooted anyway', so it seemed like a good place to perch.

Below us the crew were in party mode, as spectactors, rally officials and rival competitors handed up pieces of memorabilia for autographs. Someone in Bruce's team had discovered that the local publican was willing to trade alcohol for Brock-signed memorabilia and the boys were only too willing to trade. Didn't I explain earlier just how this crew could be amazingly innovative?

For Bruce's sake, I hope that the victory will see him move on to bigger and better things. In the past he has produced some brilliant results, but has not always been given the recognition he deserves in the sport. If anything should have come out of the PlayStation Rally it is that he does indeed have the talent, the expertise and certainly the determination to compete internationally.

At his instigation, we've talked on more than one occasion about entering a two-car team in the most famous of all off-road events, the legendary Paris-Dakar, which includes that nasty little challenge called the Sahara Desert. The enthusiasm Bruce brings to each conversation is catching, and I have happily told him that if he could put the deal together—and I would be only too happy to help—I would definitely be a starter.

This round-Australia was truly a unique event. If one part of it will always stay with me it is the fact that we all had so much fun. Sure, we took it seriously—you can't ever treat an event as tough and gruelling as a round-Australia rally lightly—but there was always time for a laugh and a joke at the end of a stage or the finish of the day.

For the first time in my motorsport career, I had the opportunity to compete in a top-class event and at the same time be able to sit back and enjoy it for what it really was—an amazing and unforgettable adventure.

Maybe Bob Carpenter summed it up the best.

'It's been tough. For that I make absolutely no apology,' he told the audience at the awards presentation. 'When Steve Frazer [the managing director of event organisers Advantage International] asked me to set up this rally, his brief was, "It's got to be tougher than '95, more competitive and it's got to have some memorable moments. I want the event to be remembered as one of the greats".

'I think the PlayStation has had all of that and more.'

So how did this one compare to the 1979 Repco for toughness? Let's first get things in perspective. The '79 event was more demanding on the motor cars of that era, which, inevitably, weren't as good as the Jackaroos of today. Admittedly, we didn't expect as much from those cars, but what we did ask of the Commodore in 1979, it delivered—far better than any other car in the event, including some four-wheel drives. And the relentless nature of the event, with the speeds you were required to do day and night, including transport sections, made it a more exhausting event for the drivers, too. After all, we did the circumnavigation in two weeks in 1979, in slower cars.

On the other hand, I was always tempted to drive faster in this event during the special stages because they were timed to the second. In 1998, you were allotted a maximum time to complete a stage, say two hours, but even so, there was a benefit in taking one hour and 50 minutes compared to one hour and 55. In 1979 we simply had to get inside a certain time. If you had two hours to complete a special stage, there was no advantage in getting there in one hour and 50 minutes. But you were penalised for taking two hours and 30 seconds.

Although some of the times set for special stages in 1979 were brutal, this difference put greater pressure on the drivers in 1998, and on the cars.

This said, in 1998, while I never backed off for one second, never once lowered my standards, I wasn't at all concerned with beating other people. I wanted to get the utmost out of the car, sure, but I also wanted to celebrate the sheer adventure and fun of getting out and having a red-hot go. Day after day for three weeks. That I did this successfully is my reward for competing in this superb event.

For a while I was thinking that it would be a good way to bow out. I'd run and damn-near almost won my second round-Australia almost two decades after the first and I'd had the time of my life. And thanks to Bob Carpenter, there were plenty of memorable moments that I would take away with me.

However, as we sat at the table at the presentation awards that night, Bob started enthusing about what he would like to do when the next event is staged. I couldn't help but feel an enthusiasm to do it all over again come over me. We'd just finished one of the toughest yet, but I reckon there wasn't a driver or crew member in the room who wouldn't have walked out of the Adelaide Convention Centre, right there and then, and jumped into their vehicles to do it all over again.

It's time I talked to Bruce Garland about what we could run the next time. Something faster I reckon, maybe a four-wheel drive ute, lots of horsepower, a different suspension system . . .

OFFICIAL ENTRY LIST

NO	ENTRANT	DRIVER	STATE	CO-DRIVER/S	STATE	VEHICLE & MODEL	GROUP
1	Rolin Motorsport	Michael Guest/Jason Walk	NSW	Jason Walk/Paul Pyyvaara	QLD	1997 Subaru Impreza WRX Sti	Gp N
2	Ian Swan	Ian Swan	VIC	Val Swan	VIC	1997 Ford Explorer	RV
3	Isuzu General Motors	Bruce Garland	NSW	Harry Suzuki	VIC	1998 Holden Jackaroo	RV
4	Warren Ridge Car Rallying	Warren Ridge	NSW	Joy Ridge	NSW	1993 Mitsubishi Pajero	RV
05	Isuzu General Motors	Peter Brock	VIC	Wayne Webster	NSW	1998 Holden Jackaroo	RV
6	Kevin Edwards	Kevin Edwards	NSW	Martin Reeves	NSW	1996 Ford Falcon XR6	PRC
8	Reg Owen	Reg Owen	VIC	Russell Cairns	VIC	1998 Nissan Patrol	RV
9	Pedders Suspension	Graeme Wise	VIC	Linda Long	NSW	1995 Holden VS Ute	PRC
12	Ross Nicastri	Ross Nicastri	NSW	Steven Green	NSW	1995 Holden Jackaroo	RV
13	Ian Swan	Steve Cornwall	VIC	Stewart Cornwall	VIC	1997 Ford Explorer	RV
14	Mark Griffith	Mark Griffith	QLD	Del Garbett	TBA	1998 Toyota RAV4	RV
15	Peter George	Peter George	VIC	Jane Oliver	VIC	1967 Datsun P510	H1
16	Daniel Castro	Daniel Castro	NSW	Anthony Hudson	NSW	1970 Datsun 1600	H2
17	Barry Rowe	Barry Rowe	VIC	Michael Ellis	VIC	1967 MGB GT	H1
18	Pedders Suspension	Ron Pedder	VIC	Scott Pedder	VIC	1995 Holden VS Ute	PRC
21	Ballarat Light Car Club	Murray Rogers	VIC	Russell McKenzie	VIC	1983 Holden VH Commodore	PRC
22	Wayne Reed	Wayne Reed	QLD	Michael O'Dea	QLD	1975 Ford Escort RS2000	H2
23	Team Bairstow Motorsport	Simon Bairstow	WA	Stephan Kulynycz	WA	1980 Datsun Stanza	PRC

LEGEND: **Gp N** Group N Rally Car; **PRC** Production Rally Car; **H1** Historic Car up to 1967; **H2** Historic Car 1968 to 1975; **RV** 4WD Recreation Vehicle

No.	Entrant	State	Driver	State	Vehicle	Class
24	Entire Building Concepts	VIC	Daniel Murphy	VIC	1982 Holden VH Commodore	PRC
			Steve Poore			
26	Peter Lockhart	QLD	Peter Lockhart	QLD	1998 Holden Jackaroo	RV
			Tim Donovan			
27	Peter Cochrane	SA	Peter Cochrane	SA	1994 Ford Falcon XR6	PRC
			Duncan Richter			
29	Andrew Smith	NSW	Andrew Smith	NSW	1980 Alfa Romeo GTV	PRC
			Andrew Smith			
30	Peter Kimpton	VIC	Peter Kimpton	VIC	1968 Ford Falcon GT	H2
			Lee Anne Griffin			
31	Alan Cameron	NSW	Alan Cameron	NSW	1972 Holden Torana LJ GTR XU1	H2
			Ted Rogers			
32	John Williams	NSW	John Williams	NSW	1969 Holden Monaro	H2
			Mike Batten			
33	Bill Monkhouse	SA	Bill Monkhouse	SA	1997 Suzuki Vitara	RV
			David Hermann			
34	Steven Phillips	TAS	Steven Phillips	TAS	1984 Toyota 4 Runner	RV
			David Phillips			
			Jason Neasy	TAS		
35	Graham Birrell	VIC	Graham Birrell	VIC	1975 Peugeot 504	H2
			Richard Pollock			
37	Garry Fitzgerald	NSW	Garry Fitzgerald	NSW	1975 Datsun 240Z	H2
			John Doble			
39	Gordon Matheson	ACT	Gordon Matheson	ACT	1968 Ford Falcon XT GT	H2
			Michael Matheson			
40	John Fraser	NSW	John Fraser	NSW	1990 Toyota Corolla FXGT	Gp N
			Gwyn Mulholland			
47	C Stewart & J Darby	QLD	John Darby	QLD	1988 Mitsubishi Galant VR4	PRC
			Col Stewart	NSW		
51	Keith Callinan	QLD	Keith Callinan	QLD	1995 Holden VR Commodore	PRC
			Paul Couper	QLD		
53	Barry Ferguson	NSW	Barry Ferguson	NSW	1976 Volkswagen Beetle	PRC
			Bret Wright			
54	Robert Gambino	NSW	David Lowe	NSW	1974 Datsun 180B SSS	PRC
			Robert Gambino			
58	Dennis Barber	NSW	Dennis Barber	NSW	1973 Peugeot 504	H2
			Andy Crane			
59	Trevor Eastwood	WA	Trevor Eastwood	WA	1968 Holden Monaro	H2
			David Hartley			
61	Michael Holloway	VIC	Michael Holloway	VIC	1969 Holden Monaro	H2
			Tim Kennon			
66	Don Williams	VIC	Don Williams	VIC	1979 Rover SDI	PRC
			Don Williams			

LEGEND: Gp N Group N Rally Car; **PRC** Production Rally Car; **H1** Historic Car up to 1967; **H2** Historic Car 1968 to 1975; **RV** 4WD Recreation Vehicle

NO	ENTRANT	DRIVER	STATE	CO-DRIVER/S	STATE	VEHICLE & MODEL	GROUP
69	Colin Hunter	Colin Hunter	QLD	Guy Basile	QLD	1998 Jeep Grand Cherokee	RV
72	Neville Hawkins	Neville Hawkins	QLD	Shirley Hawkins	QLD	1996 Toyota Landcruiser	RV
76	Michael Coates	Michael Coates	SA	Vaun Guthrie	SA	1975 Leyland P76 Targa Florio	H2
83	Humphrey Enter	Humphrey Enter	VIC	Kim Reynolds	VIC	1968 Triumph Mk 1	H2
96	Colin Hunter	Dennis McGregor	NSW	Mark Matschoss	QLD	1998 Toyota Landcruiser Utility	RV
112	Douglas Coote	Douglas Coote	WA	Cono Onofaro	WA	1966 Morris Mini Cooper S	H2
121	Dennis Sutton	Dennis Sutton	WA	David O'Neil	WA	1994 Ford Falcon XR6	PRC
144	Graham J Thompson	Graham Thompson	NSW	Matthew Thompson	NSW	1974 Volvo 144	H2
203	John Anderson	John Anderson	VIC	Peter Williams	VIC	1955 Peugeot 203C	H1
214	Gary Randall	Gary Randall	VIC	Eric Clementson	QLD	1969 Volvo 142	H2
226	Graham McPherson	Graham McPherson	QLD	Ray Scheiwe Robert Morgan	QLD	1964 Ford Fairlane Compact	H1
237	Alastair McKechnie	Alastair McKechnie	WA	John Thain	WA	1964 Holden EH Sedan	H1
240	Geoff McEwan	Geoff McEwan	WA	Andrew D'espeissis	WA	1964 Holden EH	H1
300	David Stewart	David Stewart	VIC	Graeme Rogers	VIC	1997 Ford XR6	PRC
404	Chris Hall	Chris Hall	NSW	Ron Fraser	NSW	1965 Peugeot 404	H1
505	Peter Champion	Peter Champion	QLD	Ken Long	QLD	1995 Holden VR Commodore	PRC
911	Dr Lloyd Hughes	Dr Lloyd Hughes	NSW	Peter Meddows	NSW	1972 Renault 12GL	H2
955	Eon McDonald	Eon McDonald	VIC	Victor Willman	VIC	1973 Holden LJ Torana	H2

LEGEND: **Gp N** Group N Rally Car; **PRC** Production Rally Car; **H1** Historic Car up to 1967; **H2** Historic Car 1968 to 1975; **RV** 4WD Recreation Vehicle